# A Profile of the United States Toy Industry

# A Profile of the United States Toy Industry

## *Serious Fun*

Christopher Byrne

*A Profile of the United States Toy Industry*
Copyright © Business Expert Press, LLC, 2013.
All rights reserved. No part of this publication may be reproduced, stored in a retrieval system, or transmitted in any form or by any means—electronic, mechanical, photocopy, recording, or any other except for brief quotations, not to exceed 400 words, without the prior permission of the publisher.

First published in 2013 by
Business Expert Press, LLC
222 East 46th Street, New York, NY 10017
www.businessexpertpress.com

ISBN-13: 978-1-60649-510-0 (paperback)
ISBN-13: 978-1-60649-511-7 (e-book)

Business Expert Press Industry Profiles collection

Collection ISSN: Forthcoming (print)
Collection ISSN: Forthcoming (electronic)

Cover and interior design by Exeter Premedia Services Private Ltd., Chennai, India

First edition: 2013

10 9 8 7 6 5 4 3 2 1

Printed in the United States of America.

# Abstract

The toy industry is one of the most consistently misunderstood sectors of American business. That's no surprise because on many levels it resists easy definition. It's a commodity business. No, it's a fashion business. No, it's a consumer products business. No, it's an entertainment business. The fact is it's *all* of these businesses, each of which addresses and responds to market forces differently. And often, especially with the larger, publicly traded companies—all of these businesses share a balance sheet.

Toy consumers are equally diverse, ranging from grandparents planning a splurge, to parents hoping to give their kids a leg up in learning to kids parting with their pocket change. They cross every demographic category. As we often say, if you're going to reproduce and buy stuff—or if you know someone who is—you're a toy consumer. And, those consumers have more than 160,000 different toys to choose from at any time—ranging from the hot, TV-promoted items to inexpensive impulse toys.

It's also the only industry where the performance of a multi-billion, multinational company can be largely dependent on the whims of an 8-year-old.

The toy industry in the United States is about $22 billion per year at wholesale for traditional toys, excluding video games, which are not the subject of this book. That figure, adjusted for inflation, has remained constant since the 1990s. The United States is also the largest toy market in the world, and more often than not, the trends and products that are launched here influence the global toy market. (Those products or concepts that come from overseas, notably the recent boom in Japanese Animé inspired properties, achieve global significance once they have cracked the U.S. market.) Given the stable size of the industry, the business is particularly dynamic. This year's hot company may be, as they say, sucking wind next year, depending on the product cycle. A hit product and a strong year, in other words, are neither an indicator nor a guarantee of long-term performance for any given company. The history of the contemporary toy industry is littered with companies (Coleco, Trendmasters, DSI, etc.) that grew as a result of a hit only to collapse when the hit wasn't hot. Sustainable growth over the past two decades has come from acquisitions, whether product lines or entire companies.

Given the hit and miss nature of the business, you might expect that products come and go with some regularity, and you'd be correct. Approximately 40 percent of the toys on the market in the United States each year are new introductions. There is not other consumer products business that has that level of inventory turnover in any given year.

While the industry is led by such giants as Mattel, Hasbro and LEGO, there are major players in the second tier, including LeapFrog, Spin Master, MEGA and MGA. There are also smaller companies that serve market niches or concentrate on specific channels of distribution. There are more than 600 toy companies operating in the United States. Each of these companies has different structures and strategies, and one needs to understand the various ways these companies handle operations, manufacturing, merchandising and marketing to begin to get a sense of the industry as a whole.

Entertainment companies have a huge impact as well, both in determining what kids see and want and in driving products through licensing programs. Licensing is a high stakes, competitive business, and the growth of media outlets and the Internet are changing that structure as well. The evolution of media has had, and continues to have, a profound influence on the toy industry overall, both in terms of products and marketing.

The final piece of the puzzle is retailing. Mass-market, big box retailers exert tremendous control over the industry from the products themselves to pricing to merchandising and advertising. Negotiating the complex and dynamic retail landscape is an ongoing challenge. Recent price pressures and growing competition between brick-and-mortar and online shopping as well as pressures from investors and the struggle to calibrate and predict consumer demand make this pivotal sector of the business an ongoing challenge. In addition, changes in ordering and merchandising practices continue to shift risk to the manufacturers.

While this study will focus on the U.S. toy industry, it would not be complete without an analysis of the manufacturing market in Asia, notably the Guangdong Province of China. Students of the toy industry need to understand how changes in manufacturing practices, labor, raw materials and global commodities like oil have a profound impact throughout the supply chain.

This book will provide a concise and in-depth introduction to the structure, practices and market forces that impact the toy industry. It will offer a short history of the industry, a description of the current market landscape, major and emerging industry competitors, contemporary trends, changes and expectations for the future. It will further cover aspects of retailing, consumer behavior, and financial markets as they relate to the industry. As noted, the book will focus primarily on the U.S. toy industry, but will provide guidelines for extrapolating the information to the global toy market and a highlight of those issues, such as manufacturing, that are relatively consistent worldwide.

The book is intended to provide a foundation for understanding the diverse and changing nature of the toy industry and to help readers develop a context for appreciating it relevant to other, more predictable and definable industries. Many students—and professionals for that matter—come to the toy industry ill equipped for success because they are unable to understand the various disciplines and business practices it encompasses and to apply those practices appropriately for the product or product category. A preschool toy will never behave like a toy from a hot movie. It's something many successful people in the business know and have learned over time, but it remains a mystery to the uninitiated.

This book is intended as an initiation into this fascinating, fast-paced and fiercely competitive business that is very often more an art than a science.

# Keywords

toys, toy manufacturing, toy retailing, toy merchandising, toy marketing, game manufacturing, game development, product management, operations management, Mattel, Hasbro, LeapFrog, Spin Master, VTECH, MEGA, LEGO, Toys "R" Us, Kmart/Sears, Target, Wal-Mart, Amazon, eBay, hot toys, toy retailing, toy design, toy promotion, toy consumers, toy advertising, Consumer Products Safety Commission, Toy Industry Association.

# Contents

*Acknowledgements* ...................................................................... xi
*Introduction* ............................................................................. xiii

Chapter 1   A Brief History of the U.S. Toy Industry ........................ 1

Chapter 2   The Toy Industry by Size and Category ........................ 9

Chapter 3   Product Still Rules ................................................... 69

Chapter 4   Buying and Selling .................................................. 79

Chapter 5   Creating Desire: Licensing, Advertising & Marketing ..... 95

Chapter 6   The Money Game: The Financial Realities of the
            Toy Industry ......................................................... 127

Chapter 7   So You Still Want to Play? ....................................... 137

*Epilogue* ................................................................................ 139
*Bibliography* .......................................................................... 141
*Index* .................................................................................... 143

# Acknowledgements

This book would not have been possible without the participation, support and insights of many people. First, thanks to the team at Business Experts Press who saw the potential in writing a book about the toy industry and who were enthusiastic throughout the entire process.

My agent Maryann Karinch has been invaluable in helping me organize this information and shape the project.

All the colleagues and friends in the toy industry who helped with insight, perspective, advice and the generous sharing of their knowledge and experience in the attempt to make this complex, seat-of-the-pants industry comprehensible.

They include Bernie Tenenbaum of China Cat Capital; John Barbour of LeapFrog; Neil Friedman, Greg Badishkanian and Catherine Lee of Citigroup; John Frascotti and Julie Duffy of Hasbro, Tim Kilpin and Sara Rosales of Mattel; Steve Rotter of the Rotter Creative Group, Ken Price of S-K Victory; Michael Rinzler of Wicked Cool Toys; Jerry Storch and Kathleen Waugh of Toys "R" Us; Isaac Larian of MGA; Debra Joester of the Joester/Loria Group; Michele Litzky of Litzky Public Relations; Tedd Levine, Esq. for his insights on licensing and Jim Silver of aNb Media. Their generosity with their time and their experience contributed enormously to this effort.

While all of the people named above had a direct influence on this work, there are countless people with whom I've been privileged to work over the past three decades who have experienced this business firsthand—and how maintain that's the only way to learn about this wonderful, mercurial and ever-changing business.

There's a bit of lore about this business that says that people either get into to the toy business and get out—or they become "lifers." Over my career, I've been fortunate to work with many amazing "lifers," and their collective wisdom and experience is part of what is included here as well. They also say you have to live this business to know it, and I can say that all of these people have demonstrated for me again and again that, for all its ups and downs, this is not a bad way to live.

New York—October, 2013

# Introduction

The toy industry is one of the most consistently misunderstood sectors of American business—and for those trying to get into it, it can be one of the most frustrating. Even for those who have been in it a long time, it can be virtually impossible to understand. (Indeed, many of the people whom I consulted with on writing this book assured me that it was "impossible" to write. But short of actually having a job in the business and learning in the standard "baptism-by-fire" method has characterized how most people have learned this business. Even people in the business for second and third generations in their families acknowledge that understanding it can be daunting at best.)

That's no surprise because on many levels the toy industry resists easy definition. Moreover, not only does the industry change on a regular basis in response to societal, technological, design, and manufacturing shifts, the toy industry is not, one business. It is, in fact, many different types of businesses, all under one banner.

It can behave like a commodity business in the area of basics such as balls, infant products and others.

It's also a consumer products business where companies compete to establish brands within commodity group. And, while there are comparatively few real brands in the toy business as defined traditionally—given how quickly many things come, go and change—companies still try to manage products as brands, with greater or lesser success.

It's also an entertainment business. Licensed products based on movies, television shows and other IP make up a significant sector of the business. Yet these, too, behave differently in the marketplace and can be spectacular hits—or devastating flops. As we'll see in licensing later on, no two deals are the same, and the idea of creating a template for how to do a deal can only be a guideline.

It's also a technology business. Certainly with the advent of tablet computers, iPods and smartphones of all varieties, not to mention video and online games, technology plays a bigger and bigger role in children's leisure time. Understanding appropriate uses of technology to serve a larger play experience has become a critical tool for success in this business—and one that is too often overlooked as products are rushed to market in an attempt to capture a trend.

It's also a fashion business. And we mean fashion in the larger sense. What is it about one toy that makes it a playground must-have while other similar products languish in sale bins? It is not an exact science; that's for sure. It's a combination of timing, product and the *zeitgeist*, something that can't be precisely measured or accurately predicted.

The fact is it's *all* of these businesses, and the foregoing descriptions do not even touch on the many subtleties of these sectors, each of which addresses and responds to market forces differently.

There is, however, one constant that links these different disciplines: this is a product business. At the end of the day, manufacturers must produce a good toy.

All the marketing strategy and analysis in the world is meaningless absent a good toy. But to complicate things even further, while there are some consistent elements of a "good" toy, that, too, is hard to define. Over the years, we have seen poorly manufactured products become hits, and we've seen what look like brilliant ideas fail to catch fire. In the chapter on inventing, we'll touch on some, but by no means all, of these issues.

All of this is complicated by the fact that there are no hard-and-fast rules. This is a business that has traditionally run on "gut instinct." It's been filled with spectacular successes and cataclysmic failures. The company that's riding high on a hit toy in 1 year may be pushed to the brink of bankruptcy very soon thereafter. Trying to codify this business is an enormous—and impossible—task. Why? Because just when you think that you've figured it out, something comes out of nowhere and seems to change the rules again. The standard practices of a traditional consumer products business don't apply because they're time consuming, and time is one thing that no one in the toy business really has. The business cycles are fast, making traditional research—at least statistically defensible research—impossible except in the rare cases of brands or trying to understand consumer behavior.

And if that's not complicated enough, consider this: the toy industry is the only industry where the performance of a multi-billion, multinational company can be largely dependent on the whims of an 8-year-old. It's mind-boggling to think about that in terms of a small company trying to catch a trend, but it's even more so when one considers that there are publicly traded companies where analysts are trying to forecast the business and where using traditional models will only take one so far. As noted, the company that has a mega-hit in 1 year may end up begging for sales in another.

Today's toy consumers are equally diverse, ranging from grandparents planning a splurge, to parents hoping to give their kids a leg up in learning to kids parting with their pocket change. They cross every demographic category. As we often say, if you're going to reproduce and buy stuff for the kids—or if you know someone who is—you're a toy consumer. And, those consumers have more than 160,000 different toys to choose from at any time—ranging from the hot, TV-promoted items to inexpensive impulse toys.

So…if this hasn't scared you off yet, let's dive in. Bear in mind, this relatively short book is intended only as an introduction to this complex and exciting industry. This must be read with the knowledge that the toy industry's very nature defies typical descriptions. Every product is different; every deal is different. This is a business that often tries diligently to fit into an easily comprehensible format, but it does not. As I was writing and talking to industry veterans, I repeatedly heard, "You can't write about this; you can only live it." Perhaps that's why no one has attempted this book before and why, inevitably, this book may raise more questions than it answers.

So, why would anyone really try? Because on some level the United States toy industry is the absolute embodiment of the American Dream. Someone with a good idea and a comparatively minimal investment can still make a killing—and that's what keeps people coming back. And besides, what's more fun than toys? To succeed in this business, one needs a healthy appetite for risk, a willingness to take one's lumps when they come—and they will—and the ability to get up and keep going. Because the business reflects a dynamic culture, it will never stay the same year over year.

There's one other issue that needs to be stated—and will be restated *ad nauseum* throughout the rest of this book: the toy industry reflects society; it does not lead it. Thus, it is a "lightning rod" for social criticism. This can cause endless headaches for toy companies and makes good copy for sensational news, but at the end of the day because the industry reflects the culture, it is incorrect to criticize the toy industry for creating a reflection of the culture. The root cause of an issue used to browbeat the toy business is never in the industry. Take, for instance, fashion dolls that are deemed by some to be too sexy or create bad images for children. Those dolls reflect trends seen in the larger culture and values taught in the homes. Changing the plastic totem won't address that issue.

All this being said, we're going to make the attempt to at least crack the door and provide a peak inside. If this effort is successful, it will raise as many questions as it answers. And bear in mind, as mentioned earlier, that this business will change—most likely even as you're reading this paragraph. Today's breakthrough innovation will be tomorrow's old news, but for the moment, let's leave tomorrow to its own devices and take a look at this frustrating, dynamic, and often delightful business.

CHAPTER 1

# A Brief History of the U.S. Toy Industry

1903 was a significant year in the beginning of the modern era. The first regular transatlantic radio broadcast was established. The first transcontinental auto trip was completed. (It took 3 months.) The Pepsi-Cola Company was formed, and the first Western movie premiered—"The Great Train Robbery." The Ideal Toy Company created the first Teddy Bear, named for Teddy Roosevelt.

Of course, there were always toys, but they were often made by companies in the market where the toys were sold and were generally fairly simple. Dolls, games based on classics that were neither trademarked nor patented, balls, and so forth were staples. Blocks and wooden Noah's Ark sets were also very common, though these were often created in the home. As we will see, childhood was not what it was to become. Compulsory public education began in the United States only in the early 1850s, and it took more than 60 years for that to become standard throughout the country. Children were often working with the family or on their own from a very young age. There simply wasn't the leisure that allowed play as recreation.

As a result, toys and the U.S. toy business as we know them today are distinctly a 20th Century invention. There are really four distinct "eras" of modern toy history. While these are not discreet and certainly overlap, they can help illuminate the major societal and cultural developments that have shaped childhood, toys, and play.

## The Industrial Evolution

This is really a subset of the so-called Industrial Revolution. As with everything else related to the toy industry, the adaptation of technology, such as it was at the time, lagged behind the culture at large. The commercial manufacture of toys evolved out of the larger trend toward mechanization in "grown-up" business. Beginning in the middle of the 19th Century, iron toys, wooden toys, and composition toys were the standards of American manufacturers. Many dolls were still homemade, as were puzzles, and building toys. Miniature steam engines were powered by kerosene, and boys made their own toy soldiers with small sets that allowed them to melt and pour lead. Materials were largely tin, wood, metals, and an invention from 1897—Plasticine—which was one of the earliest synthetic materials. Elaborate dolls, rocking horses, model trains, and more sophisticated toys largely came from Europe, as they would until just before World War I.

## The Growth of the American Toy Industry

In 1903, the first American Toy Fair took place in New York. It was, and for decades remained, the longest trade show of any industry for one simple reason. Enterprising American toymakers, who were not taken seriously by domestic toy merchants largely given the comparative simplicity of their wares compared to European toy makers, hoped to catch buyers before they sailed for Europe and after they returned. They would set up their stands on the docks and strove to prove that there was a market for their products and that we here in the United States could do just as well as the European manufacturers. American toy companies had to fight to get attention, but mass production and a growing population already was attracted to getting more for less and the notion that toys were something consumers actually purchased rather than made for their children was beginning to catch on. Many toys were miniatures of adult items—punch bowls, furniture sets, ironing boards—what we call role-play toys today. And mechanical toys caught the imaginations of kids who were surrounded by an ever more mechanized world. As the automobile became more widely used, pedal cars that looked like real cars became the rage. One of the major toymakers of the time was A.C. Gilbert, whose Erector sets were first manufactured in 1913. Gilbert had been inspired by the power wire towers he saw along the train lines as he traveled from New York to New Haven and was convinced that boys would want to build with miniature girders. In fact, the first Erector set book opened with the line, "Hey, boys!"—an indication of the gender divide that would define toys—and the culture at large—until the 1960s.

The child's world as a smaller reflection of the adult world had been the norm for play. After all, a child's life was all about becoming an adult. But that was all about to change.

## Post–World War II

The toys and the toy business most people know today really evolved after World War II. The post–war years were transformational in two ways. The first was technical. Advanced plastics developed for the war effort were turned to peacetime use, and in many cases that meant toys. Metal fabrication plants that had been cranking out munitions began to crank out swing sets, wagons, spring horses, and much more. Suddenly, toys were bigger, brighter, and much less expensive. As suburban moms shopped for their groceries at the supermarkets, they also had supermarkets for toys—such as Lionel Leisure, Kiddie City, and Toys "R" Us. Parents flocked to these stores because in the post–war prosperity they were able to give their children much more than they, as Depression-era kids, had been able to have.

Of course, the second major development of this period was television. As TV became standard in nearly every home, we began to have a more common cultural entertainment experience. Kids all watched the same things, and they wanted the same toys. These were the years that manufacturers like Ideal, Mattel, Remco, Gabriel, Marx, Hasbro, and many more became big players. Suddenly every child had to be Roy Rogers or Dale Evans. Howdy Doody became an icon, and the Mickey Mouse Club became the shared experience of a generation. If Captain Kangaroo had a toy on his show, you could bet that it would become a hit, such toys still made today as LEGO and Colorforms reached their first national audiences on that show. In 1958, Captain Kangaroo debuted the 64 Box of Crayola Crayons, and it became a phenomenon and a fad. Suddenly for millions of kids, their regular crayons wouldn't do.

The post–war years saw another major cultural shift. The emphasis on play began to move from practicing for adulthood to indulging in childhood. For a time, it seemed like stability was here to stay, and kids were free to just be kids. Toymakers and marketers began to realize how much money was to be made from parents who wanted to give their children the, perhaps romanticized, time of freedom and fun they felt they had missed in the Depression and the war years. At the same time, popular entertainment, the stable home, predictable life and an emerging youth culture that was distinct from—and often seen as a threat to—previous generations was emerging. Kids were beginning to control much more money and influencing purchase decisions for themselves and their families, a trend that would only be expanded upon in the coming decades. While these images were in no way representative of the entire culture and there was plenty of strife during these years, one way that kids could feel a part of it was through having the hot toy.

These years really were the beginning of the concept of the hot toy. Key items from toy manufacturers were heavily advertised on TV, and kids wanted and asked for them. The Baby Boom generation began what would become a common part of cultural history moving forward—the ability to locate oneself in time by virtue of the toys one played with.

**The Boom of Technology**—Starting in the late 1980s, chip-driven technology became a driving force in toy development. Sure, there had been some level of technology in toys before, but it was largely mechanical. Chatty Cathy, a doll that in 1959 amazed kids with the ability to say 11 different things at the pull of a string, gave way to electronic dolls that could now say hundreds. Again, toys reflected the culture, and as kids began to be surrounded by technology, they came to expect it in their toys. From learning toys to interactive, motorized stuffed animals, toys seemed alive and interacted in ways that would never have been possible.

As with what happened in the industrialization of the country, during this period as technologies evolved and some became comparatively simplistic and outdated for use in grown-up products, these chips found a new life in toys as inventors and developers found that what was no longer relevant in a computer could create a comparatively sophisticated, not to mention awe-inspiring toy. Just one example was the Furby, a fad when it was launched in 1998, was powered by one of the chips that had powered the Apple II computer 11 years earlier.

During this period, American's booming fascination with technology inspired the creation of a lot of chip-driven toys. Some like Furby or the first computer-driven game Simon from Milton Bradley did very well. Others were less successful, and some were downright disasters. This era also ushered in the rise of the so-called Watch Me toy, toys that didn't really require the participation of children to go through its paces. Though one or two became major hits, such as Tickle Me Elmo or Poo-Chi, the follow up to Furby, many of these did not and never sold.

The reason for the successes and the reasons for the failures are inextricably linked. In the case of Tickle Me Elmo and Poo-Chi, the toys became fads and owning them far outweighed the play value of the toy themselves. On the flip side, there were many inferior toys that for all the "wow factor" that developers tried to program into them, they failed to ignite kids' imaginations.

This goes back to one of the axiomatic, and elusive, elements of what makes a good toy. Technology, any technology, is never enough, the toys have to engage children. So despite the rush into the electronic world, while the construction of toys has changed, the essential role of play in child development remains unchanged. The props may change, but the function is the same. Play gives children an opportunity to explore their worlds, have new experiences (either real or imaginary), and express themselves. Those three central functions of play are not going to change, and they are essential to any successful toy.

## The Toy Industry Today

Today the toy industry is more diverse than ever before. There are more products clamoring for the "toy dollar," as it's called colloquially in reference to the money that families or kids spend on toys and related items as a portion of their overall discretionary spending, but the size of the pie remains pretty much the same. However, how it's sliced changes virtually every year. Fragmentation of the media marketplace, the rise of cable TV, and an ever-growing number of online sites—including those created by toymakers— as an entertainment destination for kids has provided distinct new challenges. From the 1950s to the late 1970s, marketers could virtually guarantee awareness, and often demand, because of the limited number of TV channels available to them. They could be reasonably sure that a significant portion of their target audience was in front of specific shows on a Saturday morning, and it was therefore incredibly easy and efficient to advertise to this group. With only three networks available and virtually no other children's programming run at other times, this was an unprecedented period for TV advertising in terms of being able to target an audience. At the same time, manufacturers could make all kinds of claims about products with none of the oversight that was to come later.

If one looks at the history of toys that were the most successful of any given year during that period, they are the ones that were most likely to have been heavily TV advertised. Today, in addition, the explosion in the number of TV shows and entire channels devoted to entertaining children—many of which have associated toy products—has made toy shelves more crowded and competitive than any time in modern history. Add to this the rise of the DVR, online programming, and home video, and it has become more complex than ever to reach a target audience with a predictable level of reach and frequency—essential components of successful marketing.

Sociological changes are also influencing the industry. Today's children, in many cases, lead highly structured lives. Between schoolwork and organized activities, our ongoing interviews with parents over the past 4 years indicate that children have less time for self-directed leisure activities, unstructured play without adult supervision, and are spending a great deal of time in transit between these activities. We'll leave it to the educators and psychologists to talk about the implications of these changes, but the implication for manufacturers and marketers is that it is harder to get attention and keep attention.

At the same time, a highly competitive retail environment is placing new pressures on manufacturers, with products having an ever-shorter window in which to establish sales performance before being yanked from the shelf. These challenges are partially offset by the growth of online retailing, which as of 2012 represented about 10% of the U.S. Toy Market and is continuing to grow at about that much annually.

Each of these issues and the ways in which they're shaping the market will be discussed in more detail in subsequent chapters.

Given all the challenges, one might easily wonder why anyone would want to get into this industry. Yes, there are tremendous risks and the chances of a huge success are relatively small.

What keeps people in the game is that this is an industry where a successful product can make people very rich and impact the culture in ways that few other products can. Moreover, compared to other industries, the barriers to entry are comparatively low. It is a business that thrives on the new, and it is one of the few businesses where anywhere from 33% to 40% of the product is completely new every year. That's a lot of risk, but at the same time it's a lot of opportunity.

Perhaps it's the lottery mentality that seems to infect U.S. culture, but people point to the successes of recent hits like Zhu Zhu Pets (a motorized hamster, which was little more than some fake fur and a bump switch), Pokémon, Beanie Babies, and others and say, "Why shouldn't I do that?"

Many of the successes defy logic, and one often hears, "Crazier things have worked," as a response to a concept that seems, at best, not strategically positioned for the market.

The challenge in trying to analyze the toy industry is that many decisions are made in ways that defy any kind of analysis. That is, by "gut instinct," "intuition," and a "feeling." In what other serious industry can the president of a company build a product line based on a dream he had? Faced with that kind of idea—and the necessary capital to make it a reality—the traditional metrics one would use to determine a product's viability in a commodity business, or even a product business targeted to adults that is not as volatile, are irrelevant.

In fact, the toy industry is not one that is run on traditional analytics or metrics. Can you imagine a major consumer product company creating a product on the basis of one person's dream? Didn't think so. At the same time, one of the reasons that this kind of activity is even possible in the toy industry is that the barriers to entry—specifically cost—are fairly low. It costs less to make a prototype and begin trying to get distribution than a major consumer product company would spend on research. There is a level of flexibility and an ability to shoot from the hip that is unique to the toy industry. Even when an idea is challenged, the standard fallback line is, "crazier things have worked," and that's an inarguable point, when one considers the myriad hits and fads that have characterized the toy business.

Larger companies, and in particular, publicly traded companies, tend to have much more systematic methods of testing markets and concepts before putting out a product, but even those don't guarantee success.

A success can come "out of nowhere," and a "sure-thing" can flop. For all the desire to turn the toy industry into a science, it really is more of an art. Bringing out a toy has more in common with making a movie than in introducing a new detergent. It is not a rational business because the toy consumer is not usually a rational purchaser. As mentioned in the introduction, billions of dollars are controlled by the changeable whims of 8-year-olds. And for the parent holding the purse strings, the motivation is seldom to invest in something of enduring value but to make a child happy in the short term, and that changes regularly as children grow.

All of this argues against any kind of formulaic or even standardized approach to trying to understand the business. At the end of the day it is, and always will be, a business driven by individual products. It has often been described as a Ferris Wheel, and anyone who has been around the business long enough has been at every point on that wheel from raking in the cash to teetering on the brink of bankruptcy. It is not a business for the faint-hearted or the risk-averse. To that end, the ride more people go on is a roller coaster.

Let's take a more detailed look at the elements of this business, and what it may be helpful to know to try to understand the constantly shifting toy landscape.

CHAPTER 2

# The Toy Industry by Size and Category

The categories of the toy industry are identified by the type of product, purchaser, and very often the end user. There are many variations within each category, and not every product fits neatly into a category. Thus, one may well ask is something a preschool toy or a learning toy? Is it both? Very often those determinations are made by the manufacturers, but the retailers may also define the categories individually. As we see so often in this business, standardization is almost impossible. Today's learning toy may have more in common with an iPad than a traditional shape alphabet block, though both may be sold in the same aisle. This chapter looks at some of the categories—as well as the exceptions—and it's a great jumping off place for trying to get a grasp on the scope of the business overall.

Interestingly, when you walk through toy stores (and there are few better ways to get a sense of the contemporary toy business than to do that), even after reading this you may be a bit confused as to why Product A is in some category. Welcome to the toy industry. Where a toy ends up merchandised in the store is often the result of competition between buyers who specialize in certain areas. These conflicts can get more and more pitched, particularly as newer toys don't always fit easily into one category or another. And yet, a significant part of the planning of any product is determining where it will go in a store—or as they say, what aisle it will go in (preschool, action figure, games, etc.)

The NPD Group is a data company based in Port Washington, New York. It's in the business of compiling data about different markets and selling it to its consumers. Founded in 1996 and with a global presence, NPD has evolved over the years. Before the advent of computerized inventory tracking at retailers, it was the only source for POS (point-of-sale) data for manufacturers. However, as retailers became more and more

**Table 2.1. State of the U.S. Toy Industry Rolling Report**

| ANNUAL DOMESTIC SALES DATA | | | | | | | | |
|---|---|---|---|---|---|---|---|---|
| SUPERCATEGORY | 2010 | 2009 | 2008 | 2007 | 2006 | 2005 | 2004 | 2003 |
| Action figures, accessories and action role play | | $1.6 B | $1.5 B | $1.5 B | $1.4 B | $1.5 B | $1.3 B | $1.3 B |
| Arts & Crafts | | 2.8 B | $2.6 B | $2.6 B | $2.7 B | $2.6 B | $2.6 B | $2.6 B |
| Building sets | | 1.1 B | $878.5 M | $699.5 M | $684.8 M | $695.8 M | $604.9 M | $581.8 M |
| Dolls | | 2.6 B | $2.7 B | $3.0 B | $3.1 B | $3.2 B | $2.8 B | $2.9 B |
| Games/Puzzles | | $2.4 B | $2.3 B | $2.3 B | $2.4 B | $2.5 B | $2.7 B | $2.7 B |
| Infant/Preschool toys | | $3 B | $3.0 B | $3.2 B | $3.4 B | $3.3 B | $3.1 B | $3.1 B |
| Youth Electronics | | $765.2 M | $917 M | $1.0 B | $1.0 B | $861.9 M | $895.5 M | $848.7 M |
| Outdoor & Sports toys | | $2.6 B | $2.7 B | $2.9 B | $2.9 B | $2.9 B | $2.9 B | $2.9 B |
| Plush | | $1.5 B | $1.7 B | $1.4 B | $1.4 B | $1.4 B | $1.6 B | $1.7 B |
| Vehicles | | $1.8 B | $1.9 B | $2.3 B | $2.1 B | $2.1 B | $2.1 B | $2.2 B |
| All other toys | | $1.4 B | $1.3 B | $1.4 B | $1.6 B | $1.6 B | $2.3 B | $2.1 B |
| TOTAL TRADITIONAL TOY INDUSTRY* | | $21.5 B | $21.6 B | $22.3 B | $22.7 B | $22.7 B | $22.9 B | $22.9 B |
| Video Games** | | $19.7 B | $21.4 B | $18.0 B | $12.5 B | $10.5 B | $9.9 B | $10.0 B |

*Source*: The NPD group / consumer panel tracking.
**Source*: The NPD group / retail tracking service.

computerized, this information was less important to get from a third party. Today, a manufacturer can sign into a retailer's site and track sales on a daily, or even hourly, basis, or however the retailer has set it up. This nearly immediate access to sales data has made the waiting for the monthly report a thing of the past. Still, NPD tracks sales and aggregates data based on consumer surveys and other methodologies, though few retailers provide their sales data.

Nonetheless, the NPD Group's tracking is the current standard for the toy industry, and while major stores no longer provide the tracking data to NPD, the company manages to provide the best overview of industry performance. Using a combination of surveys and other tools, NPD provides what the industry accepts as the most accurate possible measurement of its aggregate size. According to The NPD Group, then, U.S. domestic toy sales for traditional toys were $21.2 billion in 2011, the last full year for which complete data were available.

The following chart shows the data going back to 2003 for the overall traditional toy industry and the so-called supercategories of toys that are tracked individually.

These data illustrate the virtually flat nature of the industry both as a whole and on a category-by-category basis, but it can't begin to tell the story of the make-up of the toy business and its unique elements.

The market remains virtually constant primarily because the population of children ages 0–17 grows very slowly, approximately 1% per year, according to the U.S. Census Bureau. It is also a finite market. Toys have a role in children's lives for a very short time, particularly when considered in the context of products (cereal, soap, razor blades, etc.) that will be bought for a lifetime. Once children stop playing with toys and turn their attention to other products, that's it. They're gone as consumers. New customers are being born every year, and that offsets this annual attrition, but as noted, the birth rate is not significant enough to fundamentally alter the size of the market.

Additionally, within this population there are also significant subcategories of children defined by gender, age, and demographic profile. In its reporting, The Census Bureau breaks the child population into three age categories: 0–5, 6–11 and 12–17. Toy categories are much narrower, defined by children's physical and which are driven largely by children's physical and social development. Some may adopt a toy early and play with it longer, for instance.

And there's one more variable to consider: as noted earlier approximately 40% of the products in the toy industry are new every year. These data, while giving a reliable overview of the industry as a whole also present some challenges when one tries to analyze year-over-year data. For instance, a spike in one year in a category may not reflect a cultural trend overall but the runaway success of one product. Currently, there is no data aggregator that looks at year-over-year on such a granular level. Why? Well, for the simple reason that this data wouldn't be of much use to anyone. The short-term nature of the products in this industry and the inventory turnover mean that companies move on very quickly without too much invested in looking back and what did and didn't work. This is a business that thrives on hits, and when a hit arrives, the goal is to play it out as far as possible. That has its own levels of risk, which we'll talk about a little later on.

Thus, it's best to use this information to get an overview, as what this chart does show is that this level of constancy remains in each category even though approximately 40% of the products in the toy industry are new every year. Moreover, if we consider that there is a new generation of children approximately every 8 years, these data further underscore the constant level of toy purchases made in the United States.

Yet, technology is having an interesting impact on toys, not just in terms of adoption and use but in terms of trying to gauge the scale and trajectory of the business.

The "toy dollar," that is the money being spent on non-essential, leisure products targeted to children, is being spread across different industries. Is an iPod Touch, for instance, a toy or an electronic device? That largely depends on the individual who's using it.

In 2013, several so-called experts are trying to advance a theory that computer-based, virtual play will eventually (within the next 5 years) replace traditional toys. This is nonsense. The business growth in certain areas of traditional toys in recent years disproves this notion (as the strong performance of LEGO, Crayola and other non-electronic toys from 2010 to 2012 clearly attest), as does the constant level of sales in established categories. The role of play in child development also argues against this idea. From fine and gross motor development to social play and active play, there are many essential developmental elements that cannot be replaced by virtual play.

The bottom line is that toys always reflect their culture, as will be seen in the following sections. A Barbie from 1959, for instance, bears little resemblance to a Barbie in 2013, aside from the name. At the end of the Eisenhower years, she could be a teenage fashion model or a bride, but 54 years later, she's had more than 130 careers and reflects the virtually limitless options available to women today. A dynamic culture may be vibrant and exciting, but from a product development perspective, forecasting where the culture will be and what kids will want 2 years out is, without mincing words, impossible. This is why over the time the toy industry has been characterized by more misses than hits. Still, hits when they come can be spectacular, which is what keeps so many people in the game.

## Toy Categories

If one wants to understand the toy industry, it's imperative to understand the product, and that's a fairly tall order, which is why most people in the industry and companies for that matter tend to specialize in a given area. At their most basic level, the vast majority of toys are inert lumps of plastic, molded into a shape, put in a package and offered for sale. Naturally, what that leaves out are the emotional, intellectual and highly individual connections kids make to those toys.

There are some common features and play patterns within the individual, so-called supercategories or toys, which are helpful to understand if one is going to try to get a handle on this business. At the end of the day, however, toys are really totems onto which children project their imaginations, and the challenge for inventors, marketers and manufacturers is that no two children interact with their toys in quite the same way. While there may be overarching themes or play patterns consistent with the various categories and which toymakers hope to embody, a toy is not like a can opener or a keyboard that has a specific utility and function regardless of who is using it. Toys only have value when they inspire an imaginative experience, and that is as diverse, unpredictable and changeable as children themselves.

So, let's take a look at these categories. What follows are intended to be broad strokes introductions to these categories. We couldn't possibly touch on all the nuances and variations—sometimes by product—that impact these properties, but this is intended to give you a general introduction to these products and some of the market forces that impact these categories.

These categories are those usually tracked by the Toy Industry Association and the research group NPD. These categories have changed over time as the products have changed, so, as noted, it's virtually impossible to get an accurate year-over-year comparison of these categories. What's important to understand is how the industry breaks down the categories, always acknowledging that their size and performances will fluctuate in any given year. Indeed, as noted, one off-the-charts product can have the effect of changing the performance of an entire category as noted above. For example, the Beanie Babies fad and the first boom in Razor scooters both had a profound impact on the overall performance of plush toys and ride-on toys, respectively. It would have been tempting in those years, looking solely at numbers, to draw conclusions about category and product trends, but the performance of one product, even when it has an outsized impact on a category, cannot be interpreted to indicate a trend.

What one can count on is the cycle: the strong performance of a product in the first year will spawn a raft of imitators in the second year in an attempt to grab on to the popularity of a specific product. The market will get flooded, the boom will pass, and the category will return to more constant sales. There hasn't been a successful, breakthrough toy over the past nearly 40 years that hasn't been part of this cycle. From Trivial Pursuit launching a raft of trivia games, most of which failed while Trivial Pursuit is still on the market today, to Furby creating a category for robotic pets, to more recently the success of the app Angry Birds inspiring a flock of traditional toys based on game apps, the toy industry is one that we often say, "eats its young." The recent success of Monster High, a Mattel brand of dolls based on the imagined teenage children of classic monsters, inspired a raft of me-too product with different themes. None of them have done as well as the original, but in this business, success invites imitation—and in very short order.

Put in a less flippant and more businesslike way, this is an industry that is so characterized by risk and uncertainty that when something hits, companies rush to take advantage of it, assuming that it's a trend.

That is not to say that over the years there have not been game-changing (pun intended) products that have reshaped the industry. In the mid-1960s, designer Marvin Glass created "Mousetrap" for Ideal and started the skill-and-action game category, which uses dimensional pieces and a variety of mechanisms in the gameplay. "Dungeons and Dragons" in 1974 introduced the role-playing game, and in 1978, Milton Bradley's "Simon" was revolutionary, incorporating a computer chip into a game. These, however, are distinct from knock-offs in that they didn't try to capitalize on another company's success but rather opened up new avenues for product development.

Pokémon is a telling example of how a product can be a game-changer. Launched in the United States at Toy Fair in February 1998, the reaction of buyers was generally lukewarm. What, they wondered, was this overly complex storyline, this anime design that didn't look much like "traditional" cartoons and the whole concept of evolving monsters? Those companies that had taken a chance on the property and secured a license had a hard time getting placement. Fast forward 1 year, and buyers were overheard in the elevators saying, "I'm buying anything Pokémon." The characters had become a hit with kids. The market had spoken, and people were scrambling to catch up. Likewise Pokémon showed the market that these types of products would resonate with contemporary kids of the time, and the concept of the character-based collectible card game targeted to younger children became a new subcategory in the industry. The result, of course, is that not all products were hits, but we'll discuss this more in the chapter on licensing.

It bears repeating: the best way to understand the toy industry is to go to the toy store. You might be surprised how few people in the business spend sufficient time in the stores. It truly is the only way to understand the scope of the business, pricing strategies and the logic of some of the choices made in merchandising. We'll discuss this in more detail in the chapter on retailing, but given the turnover in the toy business, the dynamic, fashion-oriented and cyclical nature of the business, the best snapshot of the industry at any given time is what is on store shelves.

## Action Figures

### History

The Action Figure category as it's known today dates from 1964. That was the year that G.I. Joe came on the scene. Essentially, it was a doll for boys, but since no one in their right mind would buy a doll for boys at the time, a new term had to be coined. The executives at Hasbro came up with the moniker "Action Figure," and it stuck.

G.I. Joe was launched at a time when the U.S. Military was considered heroic, and the play associated with G.I. Joe and his compatriots was all about hero fantasy. The initial figures represented the Army, Navy, Air Force, and Marines, and the play was all about imagining real combat scenarios. This was consistent with TV shows of the period and certainly the national mood. The success of G.I. Joe prompted other companies to jump into the new category. The character like Johnny Hero was a sports star who could be accessorized for different sports. And 2 years after G.I. Joe, Mattel introduced Major Matt Mason, a space hero who captured the romance and adventure of the space race. The category was established, and boys' play would never be the same.

By the beginning of the 1970s, the mood in the country had changed. The Vietnam conflict had changed the attitude about the military, and these storylines were not as compelling to children. More importantly, the resistance to the draft had created an environment where military service was not aspirational or even particularly heroic, and action figure play is nothing if not heroic.

Concurrently, the Cold War spawned a new kind of hero: the secret agent. TV shows like *The Man from U.N.C.L.E.* inspired kids to imagine they were battling enemy agents. (This kind of play never really inspired action figures, *per se*. Rather, secret agent toys were more accessories and role-play toys, which were generally tracked in this category at the time.

Today, role-play has become a bigger part of the overall play pattern for boys with characters and is tracked and merchandised independently—another example of the dynamic nature of this business. What has emerged over time is that in some cases, as with the example above, kids don't want to play *with* the character, they want to imagine that they have *become* the character. While this is certainly not new in the history of play, it is only in recent years that the toy industry has invested so strongly in it as part of a character franchise—as distinct from classic role-play, such as cowboys, police, firemen, etc.)

In the 1970s with the culture in such a radical shift, if G.I. Joe was not going to fade away like an old soldier, he had to be reinvented. And he was as a "Real American Hero." He, too, became a Cold War agent and took on many more heroic guises. Enemies became more abstract, but the essential good-versus-evil play was always central to the play experience.

Throughout this period, figures based on Marvel and DC comic characters, and one-shots like Stretch Armstrong kept the market active. Mattel produced a hero line called Big Jim, which is now largely forgotten. Two highly successful characters from the 1970s were turned into action figures inspired by the real-life stunt man Evil Knievel and a figure based on the character from the television show *The Six-Million Dollar Man*.

But it was *Star Wars* that would be the game changer in this category and usher in the age of the contemporary Action Figure. Mattel declined the rights, and Kenner, a relatively small company at the time, won them. Figures based on *Star Wars* were the first in the 3 ¾-inch scale that has since become a standard in the business. Previously, figures had been more doll-like, standing between 10 and 12 inches (Major Matt Mason was about 7 inches, however), but the new, smaller size was something kids could really play with—and more importantly could afford to collect *en masse*. Kids began collecting them by the dozens. The new scale also enabled Kenner to create playsets—large plastic structures that were highly profitable and opened up new revenue potential.

The *Star Wars* success also cemented the relationship between entertainment and toys. Whereas prior to *Star Wars*, toys based on movies or television shows were at best an afterthought, toy merchandising became central to the planning of the movie, and up-front guarantees, the money paid by a toy company to secure the rights to make toys, quickly became a significant revenue opportunity for movie studios.

Throughout the 1980s, television also became a major source for driving action figure sales. G.I. Joe continued on TV, and newcomers like He-Man and the Masters of the Universe, Thundercats and more emerged as hits. And true to its nature, every toy company thought, or hoped, that it had the "next big thing," a new storyline or group of characters that kids everywhere would have to have. So today while we may remember the hits that have become part of our cultural history, for every success there were many more failures. Outside of a handful of passionate collectors, if you mentioned Coleco's Sectaurs, Mattel's Food Fighters, Hasbro's Air Raiders, or Inhumanoids or Remco's Super Naturals, you'd get a blank stare.

In fact, as we'll see in a moment, the characters that break through and become profitable, long-term successes are few and far between when compared with everything that's put out there. In the 1980s and 1990s, as *Star Wars* figures continued their dominance, Teenage Mutant Ninja Turtles, Transformers and The Mighty Morphin' Power Rangers dominated the category. Transformers, in particular, inspired all kinds of battling robots, but one ever really challenged the domination of the Autobots and the Decepticons. In fact, the failed launch of Max Steele and the Robo Force was a significant contributing factor to CBS divesting itself of its toy businesses in the mid-1980s.

### The Market Today

The Action Figure business in 2013 is characterized by several continuing hits—*Star Wars*, the relaunch of Teenage Mutant Ninja Turtles and new editions of Power Rangers.

Any significant player in this category is licensed from an entertainment property, and though there are a variety of niche products, their contribution to the category is minimal. There are also several lines of action figures that are targeted to preschoolers, but these are tracked in the preschool category.

Advances in technology have allowed manufacturers to produce figures that accurately resemble the actors the figures are based on. From

360-degree scanning to advances in molding technology, today's action figures are more detailed than ever before. One needs to only compare the original *Star Wars* figures to those made today to see the advances over the past three decades. This verisimilitude is important to collectors as well, and figures such as those based on WWE wrestlers gain in value based on the accuracy of their reproduction. They also gain in cost. The cost of scanning and sculpting adds to the cost of the figures, as do licensing fees with personalities as well as properties. Carrie Fisher, for example, has publicly acknowledged that she never licensed her likeness at Princess Leia in *Star Wars*, and so has lost out on royalty revenue. However, the widespread licensing of likeness began about the time of *Star Wars*, and so today, for example, the new Roadblock figures based on *G.I. Joe Retaliation* bear a striking resemblance to the actor Dwayne Johnson who plays him in the film. Even with these additional costs, however, the price of individual action figures has actually decreased when the effects of inflation are factored in. For instance, the original Star Wars figures cost approximately $3.99 in 1979. That would be about $15 in 2013 dollars, which is significantly more than the $7.99-$9.99 (depending on features) that these figures go for in 2013.

In 2013, the traditional, static, action figure is also being challenged by new play formats. Activision's Skylanders, for example, combine electronics and video game play with traditional action figure play and collecting. These figures when placed on a gaming or computer peripheral appear as digital images in a video game. In 2012, Skylanders was the best-selling action figure in the United States, even without counting sales of the game. At the same time, LEGO continues to expand its licenses and proprietary stories and characters to eat into traditional action figure sales. While LEGO figures may more regularly be tracked in the construction toy category, they are still taking a percentage of the toy dollar that would have gone into more traditional action figures.

Additionally, fragmentation of the media marketplace and the proliferation of TV programming targeting boys has created many new opportunities for toymakers to produce product, but the competition for boys' attention—and dollars—is greater than ever before. The inspiration for these toys has shifted to television and away from movies, as a child who is a fan of a particular show or set of characters is more likely to be immersed in them through daily TV watching and then more likely to want to reflect that in his play.

At the same time, there has been a shift in the way in which boys play with these characters. There is a greater emphasis, as noted earlier, on role-play toys as boys' play is more about becoming the characters than playing with them. When the original Harry Potter movies came out, for example, action figures of the characters didn't do so well, but there was a decent business in toys that allowed kids to feel like they were in the story.

But kids do not respond to every property in the same way. In 2013, the relaunch of the Teenage Mutant Ninja Turtles has been highly successful from Nickelodeon for several reasons. First, Nickelodeon controls the airwaves and can put the show on as much as they choose to, driving it into kids' consciousness. (This strategy also worked with Cartoon Network who made a success out of its Ben 10 toy lines.) The Turtles toys from Playmates have been successful in both action figures and role-play toys because the potential market is large enough to accommodate individual children's play styles.

### *How the Current Market Behaves*

Today, the market is highly entertainment driven, and that entertainment comes primarily from television. As noted previously, when a show comes into the home 5 days a week, boys' engagement is higher than in a movie. In addition, the prevalence of DVR recording and other forms of home video means that for kids who are engaged by a particular character or line of characters the opportunity for repeat viewing is greatly enhanced.

Television also offers the opportunity of year-round sales as opposed to movies that have about a 6-week window for retailer in advance of a movie's opening. With some larger entertainment franchises, the combination of media only strengthens a property, but that's not always possible.

Still, one of the most prevalent current strategies for action figure manufacturers is what we'll call franchise building. Increasingly, a movie is seen as an event in the life of a character, not the main—and sole—foundation for toy sales. Take, for instance, Batman as one example. The recent movies have been wildly successful at the box office internationally. They have also been fairly dark and rated PG-13, which means that the vast majority of the children who will be playing with the toys are unlikely to see the movies. There are, therefore, different iterations of Batman in the marketplace. Fisher-Price, for instance, makes a Batman in its preschool playset line that is much more appropriate to a preschooler. Still, it is Batman, and through these toys a child gets to participate in the cultural excitement surrounding the character, yet in a way that is age-appropriate for him or her. Batman also has a TV show and other media targeted to kids, so they are involved with the property while the culture is as well. These toys also have the benefit of providing revenue for manufacturers and retailers even as the typical 6-week window for a movie has passed. Hasbro has used the same strategy with Spider-Man and *Star Wars* toys, trying to find strategic ways to keep kids engaged with a property while at the same time capitalizing on the awareness building impact of a movie in the wider culture.

Action Figure play is open-ended, narrative-based play. That is, kids are engaged in the characters and the storylines as presented in the entertainment. However, the subsequent play doesn't always replicate what's seen on the screen. Rather, kids interpret the characters into their own scenarios that reflect their individual personalities. But the story is key to kids' engagement and adopting the characters and narratives into their play, and though the details may be slightly different in each expression of the story, the fundamental play pattern of action figures is power and conflict. This is a dynamic that is inherent in boys' play, and at least until boys' development process changes, will stay constant.

The core age for action figure play is age 4–6 years, though in some cases it may go as high as 8, but there are many developmental stages within that range. Typically, there are properties that appeal to the younger end of the age group (currently Power Rangers, Spider-Man, and Batman, for example) and properties that appeal to the older end (currently Star Wars, Teenage Mutant Turtles and Mattel's 2013 introduction Max Steel). While it is in some ways a generalization, boys at the younger end of the age spectrum tend to fantasize about having super powers as a response to a world that's controlled by adults while older children tend to appreciate more sophisticated and nuanced storylines. Boys, then, move from one type of character to another as they get older and their play reflects their intellectual and emotional development. (We'll see a similar progression with girls and dolls in that category.)

At the same time, established properties will tend to "age down," meaning attract younger kids than it might have originally because playing with those toys is associated with being "bigger," something that kids naturally want.

## Transformers: Three Decades of Success

Transformers, first introduced by Hasbro in 1984, was a classic good-versus-evil story of the never-ending battles between the good-guy Autobots led by Optimus Prime and the bad-guy Decepticons led by Megatron.

The original transforming toys (from vehicle to character robot) were licensed from Takara, but it was Hasbro that developed the storylines and the various entertainment platforms. A TV show, comic books and later animated movies drove the storyline into boys' lives, and the larger-than-life robots who gave power to the humans that interacted with them was a classic theme and play pattern for boys ages 6 and up. The manipulative play of transforming the robots was certainly part of the appeal of the toys in the early years.

Over time, the stories became more sophisticated, and an entire mythology around the characters developed. This had the effect of aging up the property for kids who wanted a more sophisticated storyline, while the cartoon shows engaged the younger end. Hasbro effectively engaged both ends of the consumer universe in age- and developmentally appropriate ways.

Hasbro also created toys with different levels of sophistication so that younger kids could engage with a transforming experience that was simple and easy for them to do.

The constant introduction of new themes (a strategy the Power Rangers have used to good advantage as well) kept the storylines fresh as new children grew into the property. Over time, the Transformers became known even among kids who never played with them, and 20 years into the property, a second generation was beginning to discover them.

Finally, three successful live-action movies continued to broaden the franchise and drive toy sales at the upper end of the age spectrum—and adults—even as an ongoing television show entertains the younger kids. There are different ways for kids to interact with the Transformers at different times and still have what is, to them, a satisfying experience with the property.

Moreover, as with many mature entertainment properties, a movie is an event in the life of the franchise. It is not a make-or-break experience. Indeed, with the movies rated PG-13, there are many kids at the younger end of the Transformers audience who won't see it, and yet they are engaged in the property through the TV show and some of the toys and so are engaged in the cultural excitement that surrounds a blockbuster movie.

Toy sales in a movie year are going to be significantly higher than in non-movie years, so the strategic challenge for a company like Hasbro is certainly to manage the franchise so that it remains strong on its own but also to manage the entire product portfolio to account for the inevitable highs and lows that come with a mature property.

Few properties will ever achieve the track record Transformers have had. They have passed from playthings into parts of our larger culture. Far more common is an action figure line that lasts 2–3 years and appeals to a core audience while they are in that target age bracket. Inevitably, kids—and the market—demand something new. It is also a rare property that can be re-launched and find an audience. Teenage Mutant Ninja Turtles has done it, but He-Man was unable to. It's a combination of timing, promotion and, of course promotion.

### Action Figures—What It Takes To Succeed

An entertainment platform is essential to the success of a contemporary action figure line. As previously stated, the story has to be compelling enough that kids will not merely want to watch it but that they will want to express themselves through play with the characters.

And it has to remain top-of-mind with the target audience. There are only too many characters waiting in the wings, so to speak, ready to duke it out for any market share that isn't promoted and protected. The scale and nature of the entertainment platform will in part determine the size of the program. A television show that's shown 5 days a week for a year is more likely to have a longer-term toy potential than a movie that has approximately a 6-week window to attract an audience.

It's not that one of these necessarily offers more potential than the other, it's that the profitability has to be calculated based on the nature of the program. Even so, at the end of the day, a movie or TV show that bombs is not going to sell any toys, so the stakes are high, particularly as commitments to produce toys and licensing contracts are often signed well in advance of the entertainment being finished.

Other factors can also impact action figure sales. In 2012, for example, Paramount announced that it was postponing the release of *G.I. Joe: Retaliation* from June to March of 2013 in order to reshoot scenes after poor responses to early test screenings. This is never a good sign, and in this case Hasbro (which also owns the intellectual property and had a major producing role in the film) had already shipped some product, but held back on more of it. The loss of sales and costs of holding inventory for 9 months were somewhat offset by strong sales of other Hasbro entertainment toys, but at the same time a movie released in the summer has traditionally sold more toys than one released in the spring. The purpose of this is not to analyze Hasbro's finances related to these toys but to highlight the unpredictable nature of this business and the impact that factors not necessarily in the control of a toy company can have on the business.

Television programs have a slightly easier time of it, but only slightly. Here there is the opportunity to wait and see if a show develops a fan base and a demand for product prior to making a full commitment to product. While there is still investment cost in design and preparing to manufacture, losses can be mitigated if a show doesn't perform. Conversely, if a show is a success, rolling product into the market on an ongoing basis keeps supply lagging behind demand, and that can have a positive impact on the longer-term potential of a property.

In the current market, television also offers expanded partnership opportunities between toy companies and content producers. Whereas traditionally networks would pay a fee to be able to air content, and the content provider would own the property, be responsible for production costs and get the licensing revenue from toys and other products, more and more were seeing different kinds of deals being struck. As more and more children's television watching shifted to cable and such channels as Cartoon Network, Nickelodeon and others, the fees networks paid didn't cover the cost of producing the entertainment. Content producers became more and more dependent on revenues from licensing and other promotional deals to generate revenue from a property to offset production costs and be profitable. What we've seen in recent years are deals where the network also becomes a producer on the project and shares in the revenue. One illustrative example of this has been *Ben-10* created by Cartoon Network. They own all the content, and since they own the airtime could do things like created *Ben-10* Marathons, which helped jumpstart the property with kids, which in turn drove product sales. Similarly, as toy companies are developing their own intellectual property, they can go into partnership with broadcasters, or they can pay the broadcasters to air the program, as part of the marketing of the property.

The collector market drives a certain amount of action figure sales as well. Properties like WWE (World Wrestling Entertainment) appeal largely to the adult male collector, ages 18–34. This market behaves differently than other parts of the action figure sector in that the avid fans will buy often and deeply. The challenge is to keep refreshing the market place, sometimes on as short as a 6-week cycle.

Collectors have certainly driven—and continue to drive—the expansion of the *Star Wars* line. Thousands of different figures have been created, but ironically, this brand behaves more like a commodity than other parts of the Action Figure category because a long history allows Hasbro to project sales with a certain level of accuracy and determine viability and profitability of any new figures—to an extent at least. The strong collector universe, however, is quick to express what they'd like to see as figures.

Yet not every property is going to inspire rabid, passionate collecting. Take *The Lord of the Rings*, for example. While that had a tremendous fan base, gauging the potential market for action figures was a challenge. They never achieved what many assumed was going to be its mass market potential. While some collectors bought into it and were quite active in discussing the details of the costumes and decorations on the figures, they did not drive sufficient sales. At the end of the day, there was really no way to play *Lord of the Rings*, and so the items failed as toys.

And that's a critical question, particularly in this category. Whether a figure is for collecting or playing, the one thing every action figure line requires is what we call a "way in." With collectors that means a story that resonates so personally deeply that fans want to reflect that connection in purchasing figures for display. With kids, it means that the story is compelling enough that they want to play it.

In the latter case, and assuming that you have a great story that kids will want to watch, the next question that too few manufacturers ask (or answer honestly when there is potential revenue at stake) is: How will kids play it? Cute as the monsters were in *Men In Black*, for example, there really was no way for kids to play it because it was just about blasting monsters, *and* kids weren't sufficiently immersed in the storyline or the main characters that they wanted to play out their versions of the storyline. On the other hand, the Teenage Mutant Ninja Turtles in their unending battles with the character Shredder and the Foot Clan provide ongoing fodder for kids' active imagination and play. It's not enough merely to have a plastic representation of a character; kids must also be able to project themselves into their version of the narrative.

The other questions that must be asked when launching an action figure line is: What are you bumping off the retail shelf and, equally importantly, what are kids going to put down in order to pick up your product. (This is not just relevant to the action figure category; it applies to the toy industry as a whole, but it has particular resonance for this category.)

The two questions are interrelated. The first is fundamental to being successful in getting placement with retailers. It requires knowing where the competition is in its life cycle what your figure offers and an ability to project greater revenue per square foot of shelf space than the competition.

In the case of some movie toys, the challenge may be a little easier because when one movie goes another comes in and that shelf space is more easily allocated. In the case of a television show, for instance, the challenge is to show the potential for staying power, which is the rational for trying to build a character franchise with different versions of the same category discussed earlier. A retailer that is making a satisfactory margin on a property is unlikely to give that up for something untested. (We'll discuss this more in a subsequent chapter on sales.)

With kids, time and attrition will work in your favor. Kids grow out of and get tired of properties and the next crop of kids coming up often wants something new, but with properties that are continuing to reinvent themselves and appealing to new generations of kids, the challenge becomes somewhat greater.

If all of this sounds a bit confusing and inexact, that's because it is. As we will continue to see, there are no hard-and-fast rules as to what will work. Excitement about a television show or a movie can be tremendous before it debuts or airs, and manufacturers and retailers can make multi-million dollar commitments based on the belief that something will be good. In this way, the toy industry is exactly like the movie industry; there is a level of belief that is based on the conviction of an individual or a group, but there is no way to determine how the market will respond until the product is out in the public. The only way to mitigate risk is to do less, but that risks leaving money on the table that one won't get back. Hence, there is the go-big-or-go-home mentality when it comes to signing up some movie properties for toys. A property may do well enough so that no one loses money. It may be a spectacular failure or it may so far exceed expectations that it becomes a cash cow for decades. The flip side of that is always the movie that didn't have sufficient merchandising and then became a big hit, only to disappoint in terms of sequels. *Shrek* was a tremendous hit with kids and families, though it wasn't heavily merchandised. When *Shrek 2* came along, the assumption was that if there had been toys they would have done well. They didn't because while kids loved the movies, they didn't want to replicate the movie in their play. Not all kids movies make good toys. We'll talk more about this in the chapter on licensing.

Remember, major companies with experienced people didn't believe that *Star Wars* or *Toy Story* for that matter had sufficient potential to sell toys to make it worth the risk.

## Arts And Crafts

### *History*

The basic products of arts & crafts—crayons, paints, etc.—have been staples for centuries. As toys, though, the modern era is generally dated from 1903 when Crayola introduced its first box of eight colored crayons.

(Previously, Binney & Smith had made black wax crayons only.) Sold as art supplies and in various kits over the years, these have not really changed much. Innovations, such as paint-by-number, and other innovations made "professional" results possible for kids. Other innovations have never varied too much from the basic coloring, painting and collage play.

Highlights of the post–World-War II years included Kenner's Sparkle Paints in the early 1960s that allowed kids to make pictures that, you guessed it, sparkled. Crayola introduced the aforementioned and now-classic 64-crayon box in 1958. The rise of electric toys made such hits as Mattel's Vac-U-Form and Creepy Crawlers. (Creepy Crawlers has been successfully reintroduced several times since.) Shrinky Dinks fascinated kids and crafters alike. Typically when these products were advertised heavily on television, they did well. For the most part, though, the arts & crafts (and we include activity toys in this category as well) sector has been a staple category that doesn't require much promotion, given that it's a very basic way kids play. This has allowed manufacturers to deliver products with high margins and year-round sales.

## The Market Today

The arts & crafts market has been fairly stable representing about 12% of the U.S. toy market over the past decade. As noted above, these products sell year-round, with increased sales during the late-July-through-August Back-to-School shopping season.

The stability of this category is also significant in an environment where electronic toys, tablets and Smartphones have continued to grow and be used by younger and younger children. Part of this is parents' ongoing desire to limit screen time, but it also speaks to the classic nature of this kind of play.

Recent innovations have focused on limiting mess, which many companies realized was a primary concern of moms. Such products as Crayola's Color Wonder, where the paints or markers show up only on special paper, have been very successful. Complete sets that allow kids to make specific items have also attracted older kids.

Finding ways to create new opportunities for purchase and new materials have also driven the category. Adding features such as lights and sound to drawing tablets, configurations that make take-along play easier and providing new playsets with different themes, all give parents a reason to purchase more deeply.

Play-Doh is an excellent example. First introduced in 1956, the compound has remained relatively unchanged over the years. However, finding different ways to mold and make things that look finished has been a challenge. From its first Fun Factory to the recent reformulation of Play-Doh Plus (a smoother more easily molded adaptation) along with the original, these inspire multiple purchases within the individual household.

And that's really one of the key characteristics of this category: these products are consumable. Crayola estimates that by the time a child reaches the age of 6 he or she will have gone through, on average, about 700 crayons.

This is also a category that is not as limited when it comes to age. Children as young as 18 months can play with crayons, and various craft sets can appeal to kids as old as 10. Other recent trends have incorporated creating fashion and décor accessories, popular licenses and materials that have included plastic gems and duct tape. The fashion-oriented segment of this business seeks to replicate current fashions and interpret them for younger kids.

Licensing certainly plays a role in this category and particularly in the consumable segment. This allows kids to engage with characters without a huge investment by parents, and at the same time because these products are often easy to produce and often involve only printing, the barrier to entry for many manufacturers is fairly low.

From a retail perspective, both the year-round nature of this category and comparatively high margins are appealing. While mass-market retail is dominated by a few players, the specialty market (See the discussion of this in the chapter on retailing.) carries a great many more of these products. There are also dedicated stores such as Michael's and Hobby Lobby that buy these types of toys and almost no other categories of toys. These stores appeal to crafters and carry much more than toys, but they do a strong business in arts and crafts toys, as you might assume given that if an adult in the family is engaged in these types of activities their children may be as well.

In addition to Crayola, there are several key players in this category. MEGA's Rose Art line has recently invested in expanding and refining the play experiences. Alex has a wide range of products known for their quality and play value. Relative newcomer Fashion Angels has successfully established itself with older kids through its own brand and licensing deals with brands such as Project Runway and Mattel's Monster High, as well as through its innovative use of materials like duct tape. However, there are more than 85 companies of varying sizes that play in this diverse category.

### *Arts and Crafts—What It Takes To Succeed*

As noted, the barriers to entry can be comparatively low in terms of manufacturing costs, and the products are often commoditized. Modeling compounds, chalk, markers, paint, crayons and so forth do vary in terms of quality, but the consumable nature of these products and the relatively low retail price points tend to make consumers less discriminating if they think something is going to be fun for their kids. (Many parents say that what they're buying with these sets are not just products their kids will enjoy but "quiet time for me.") Still, there is a great deal of brand loyalty to brands like Alex, Rose Art or Crayola, as parents consistently report that they have had positive experiences with their products over time.

The real opportunities for success in this category involve leveraging consumable commodities in new ways that enhance play. Hasbro, for example, has consistently done well with the Play-Doh sets that involve creating food products. In addition to creating more mess-free products, Crayola looks for new ways to leverage compounds and incorporate different play experiences, such as games or narrative play, into the arts and crafts experience. Still, getting retail distribution can be a challenge, so a strong license can help, though that will add to the costs.

Also, since the majority of these products are not TV advertised, packaging plays a pivotal role. In addition to making the products look fun, high piece count, number of projects one can create, and the ability to purchase refill kits all factor into this. One of the most important factors is to understand the cognitive and physical abilities of children who are using these products.

# Building and Construction Sets

## *History*

The beginning of the 20th Century was a huge time for construction toys. A building boom was going on in the country, and so naturally that would be reflected in toys. In 1913, the first Erector sets were launched. The following year, Tinkertoy made its debut. And in 1918, Lincoln Logs first appeared. All three of these are still made today. As are basic blocks, which have been around for centuries, but they started being made and marketed as educational tools in the late 18th Century.

Construction serves a wide variety of developmental purposes, from encouraging eye-hand coordination, to building spatial relationships, enhancing perceptual acuity and understanding other elements of the physical world. Generations of children have been—and continue to be— fascinated by the building process.

While some of the relatively modern toys were marketed heavily to boys, such as Erector sets, this kind of play is inherently gender neutral and its benefits have been well documented as children imagined, built, destroyed and built again.

As toys, the three mentioned above dominated the industry through the first half of the century. In 1947, a Danish company introduced interlocking bricks called LEGO and while they made a small success in Europe, it wasn't until in 1960 the then-president of Samsonite luggage introduced them to the United States that LEGO began to take off.

Various different configurations of toys were introduced, and people may remember American Bricks, Capsela and others, but by the 1970s, LEGO was the dominant construction toy on the market, and brick-based building became the standard. Many companies got into the block market, including Best-Lock in England, Coko in China and Mega Bloks in Canada, and as LEGO's patents expired between 1978 and 1989, the company was involved in lawsuits trying to prevent other companies from making them. The final ruling that the bricks were functional and therefore could not be trademarked came in Canada in 2005. As you'll see in a moment, this event which might have sunk another company has instead had little impact on LEGO as it continues to report growth at a rate far outstripping any other toy company.

The only other major construction system to be introduced and demonstrate any staying power has been K'NEX. First introduced in 1993, the system of rods and connectors was certainly reminiscent of Tinkertoy, but its design allowed for more versatile building.

However, few categories illustrate the cyclical nature of the toy industry more dramatically than the construction category. By 2003, the category was in decline, and LEGO suffered losses. Hasbro had attempted to get into the market with a block-based building system that year, which failed to catch fire. The entire category had declined to about $600 MM in sales in the United States.

It's impossible to pinpoint an exact cause of the turnaround in this category. Yet, licensing and entertainment certainly played a part—as did the expansion in the mass market. LEGO, which had never produced licensed construction sets and would certainly have been vulnerable to another company experienced in licensing mounting a competitive system, began producing *Star Wars* sets since 1999, and as the category started to recover, licensing and niche products would play an increasingly larger role in its growth. (Ironically, Hasbro had had the chance to get into the construction sector with the *Star Wars* license and passed on the deal. When LEGO picked up the license, it saved the company and set the stage for its later growth.) Suddenly, kids who would not necessarily participate in open-ended building were deeply engaged in LEGO because of *Star Wars* and many licenses that would follow. Today, LEGO represents about 85% of the entire construction category.

At the same time, Mega Bloks continued to grow and more and more kids started building. Themed sets became more and more prevalent, and fans would buy deeply in a specific line. Yes, you could still buy a bunch of bricks, but the trend became much more about building specific models, and the elements of good construction toys—build, play, display—figured more and more in the design.

## The Market Today

With revenues nearly triple what they were in 2003, building and construction toys are a hot category.

Several things are driving this growth, probably the most significant contributing factor is that companies like Mega Bloks and LEGO have successfully broadened the potential audience. While building was at one time limited to open-ended play, the boom in licensed properties and the transition to a more theme- and model-based play pattern has brought new people into the fold.

*Star Wars* continues to be huge for LEGO, but LEGO has also successfully introduced its own intellectual property that it has promoted not merely through building sets but through online entertainment and highly developed storylines. The company branched out into the gaming category and took a bite out of that category. With properties based on movies and television shows, LEGO also has taken share away from the action figure category.

Similarly, Mega Bloks has continued to grow with niche products like lines based on the video game *Halo*, as well as developing lines based on other properties and franchises. While these may be niche properties, they provide a compelling reason for their fans to purchase. Hasbro, rather than licensing its G.I. Joe and Battleship properties to either LEGO or Mega Bloks, developed its own line called KRE-O, which has been a modest success and additional revenue in these properties that they control. Hasbro had an interesting decision to make in launching this line. Certainly, they could have licensed their intellectual property to either LEGO or Mega Bloks, but having made a foray into the construction category in 2003 and 2004 with a short-lived line called BTR (Built to Rule), the company had some experience in the category and chose to market its lines to fans who like construction as one element of their entire brand portfolio. They could be the only fish in Hasbro's construction category sea, to speak metaphorically, rather than being a secondary or tertiary line as a licensee.

Contemporary construction sets go beyond model building, and companies have learned that a successful toy in this category also needs to deliver more elements of play and "playability" than would have been more common in 1990s and earlier. To add value to the sets, kids want vehicles that they can play with and figures they can imagine in different scenarios. Traditional play patterns complementing the construction, whether in open-ended narrative play, or to a lesser degree, games, have contributed to success. Whether under a license or as a stand-alone property, kids are also buying across a franchise, complementing major birthday or holiday purchases of expensive sets with lower cost sets that are bought year-round. The boom of these sets has turned this into a year-round purchase. Additionally, the figures have become collectibles, particularly when they are done in the likeness of popular characters, and there are some LEGO fans that are almost exclusively into collecting these figures. (There are more LEGO minifigures in existence than there are people on the planet.)

Both LEGO and Mega Bloks have continued to expand their preschool and young builder lines as well, further broadening their potential market and creating product targeting a discreet market segment. These toys are more preschool in nature, focusing on blocks that are easy for small hands to grasp and manipulate and simple builds. However, they are marketed and merchandised as construction, or more accurately, preschool construction, a sub-category.

The big news, though, in 2012 and 2013 has been the expansion into the girls' category. LEGO introduced its Friends line and Mega announced a line of Barbie building sets, developed with and licensed from Mattel. The introduction sparked controversy about LEGO trying to pander to gender stereotypes by giving girls dollhouses and making the pieces pink, but the fact of the matter has been that 80% of LEGO toys had been sold to boys. There are plenty of girls who are, and have been, engaged in more traditional construction play and who respond to the LEGO *Star Wars* and LEGO City lines as well as some of the other collections. However, after 3 years of research, LEGO determined that while there are many girls who enjoy construction play, the themes and pieces didn't appeal to them as much. LEGO Friends made a strong debut and continues to do well. Likewise Mega Blok's Build 'n Style Barbie sets have done well after a late 2012 introduction and a larger roll-out in 2013. Interestingly, there are several small companies who are trying to get into this category, such as GoldieBlox that was funded via Kickstarter, but as of mid-2013, they have yet to make any significant inroads, since both LEGO and Mega Bloks are sold throughout all retail channels.

The growth in this category has been possible because between expanded licensing deals and opening new markets, it has continued to grow without cannibalizing existing business. This category is also unique in that fans tend to stay in it longer and some become lifelong users. While there is certainly attrition and the adult construction consumer market is comparatively small, it nonetheless contributes to the category's overall performance.

### *Building and Construction—What It Takes To Succeed*

The barriers to entry are quite high in this category. Design and engineering costs are high, and consumers are very sensitive to performance. Systems need to work, and bricks need to stay together. Quality is a paramount issue to parents, particularly as more and more active play is integrated into these products. Moreover, between LEGO and Mega Bloks, most of the top-shelf properties appropriate for this category have been secured across all demographic groups, literally closing out other companies who might want to get into this sector in a brick system.

In addition, creating a new system is challenging, given the amount that individual consumers invest over time. There is a greater potential for success in creating systems that work with "other brick-based building systems," as the marketing lines go. In creating KRE-O, Hasbro created a system that would integrate with LEGO while leveraging its own intellectual properties. The strategic choice was whether to license their intellectual property to a building toy company or incur the expense of design and production with the potential to generate more revenue. They chose the latter course. Mattel, on the other hand, chose to license its Barbie and Hot Wheels properties to Mega Bloks. There is no right or wrong strategy here; it's simply a matter of determining what's the best revenue potential for a property and, of course, always acknowledging that there are no guarantees.

While K'NEX has been a consistent seller, its market is smaller. Reintroductions of Tinkertoy (including a pink version targeting girls) and Lincoln Logs pick up small pieces of the market. Smaller companies have introduced other systems, such as CitiBlocs, which is a variation on a classic wooden block, but these have limited appeal and are generally a parent-driven purchase based on perceived educational value. Likewise systems like Zoob and Uberstix, both of which have unique designs and marketing platforms, receive many awards and accolades and can be profitable, but they are not mass-market toys.

All of this said, the recent success of the category has prompted many companies of all sizes to look at getting into the market. While nothing is ever written in stone, the best opportunities for a mass-market success are going to be those that integrate with brick-based systems and capitalize on the momentum of the marketplace while providing innovation. The reality is that consumers tend to buy deeply in these categories, and the demand for new sets and configurations is great. There are some brands that are targeted to specialty stores, and companies like Hape make beautiful wooden sets, but these have a much smaller share of the market in the United States than the leading brands. That doesn't seem likely to change any time soon.

## Dolls

### *History*

Dolls, along with balls, tops and others, are among the oldest playthings known to human civilization. Volumes have been written on the development of dolls and the history of dolls. Moreover, the essential play of dolls has remained unchanged over centuries. In the contemporary world, doll play breaks down fairly easily into a few specific play patterns. Nurturing play is a role-play activity in which girls see themselves as mommies, taking care of a baby. Fantasy play surrounds narratives that incorporate supernatural beings—fairies and other magical beings. Fashion doll play is aspirational in nature, but it, too, breaks down into specific segments. Also included in this segment are mini dolls, dolls based on animals such as Hasbro's My Little Pony or Littlest Pet Shop brands.

The doll sector as we know it today emerged after World War II. Dolls had primarily been baby dolls, though there were phenomena such as the Shirley Temple doll. Fashion dolls were limited and were primarily paper dolls, though Betsy McCall (based on McCall's magazine) was a 6-year old. The play was either about being a mommy or having a best friend. All that changed in 1959 with the introduction of Barbie. Called a "Teenage Fashion Model," this was the first plastic doll onto which girls projected their fantasies about being older, individuals and independent. Still, baby dolls persisted as Ideal introduced various feature dolls such as Betsy Wetsy, Tiny Tears and Thumbelina that all did something—pee, cry, move—and, of course, Mattel's Chatty Cathy, the first talking doll who said an amazing 11 different things. (Chatty Cathy was one of the best-selling dolls in the United States from 1959 to 1965. It was later reintroduced in 1970, though it was not as successful in its relaunch.)

From the mid-1960s on, the so-called feature doll became an annual offering. Beautiful Crissy had hair that grew. Baby Alive in the early 1970s actually pooped out the gelatinous green food girls fed her, and as technology improved, dolls did more. By the late 1990s, dolls like Playmates Amazing Amy were powered by a computer chip, cost nearly $100, and were intended to be the most realistic nurturing experience possible. (Just over a decade later, these dolls look clunky and unsophisticated with children having to make a connection between, for instance, a feeding spoon and the dolls mouth by matching metal contacts. Still, at the time, it seemed quite advanced.) However, as the economy changed and certainly after the economic impact of the recession that began in 2007, manufacturers were challenged to come up with feature dolls that were less costly to consumers. Concurrently, consumers were staging a mini backlash against these dolls, saying that they simply wanted a simpler doll. Still, when Hasbro re-released Baby Alive in 2006, the doll was one of the hits of the year, yet another indication of how unpredictable the toy business can be—and how much a single product can influence it.

Barbie meanwhile went through her ups and downs, almost disappearing in the early 1970s as women's roles and gender perceptions changed. In the early 1980s, a young and brilliant product manager named Jill Barad and then Mattel CEO, John Amerman, virtually reinvented Barbie and started her on the road to the leadership position she has in fashion dolls today. Barbie's long and colorful history has been documented in other works, but for those wanting to learn about the toy market, the important thing to remember as one looks at Barbie is that her ongoing viability has come from being reinvented as the market has changed. She may be a cultural icon, but she has always had to appeal to contemporary children in the contexts of their worlds.

### The Doll Market Today

The doll market is usually broken up into six distinct segments, each of which has different behaviors in the market. These six represent the categories as defined by most retailers and manufacturers with an emphasis on the mass market. Not included in this are stand-alone brands like Mattel's American Girl, which is unique in the market in that Mattel handles all manufacturing, marketing and retail. Also not included here are the limited market collectible dolls made by hundreds of small companies and individual artisans.

## Baby Dolls

Baby dolls run the gamut from basic, inexpensive unbranded dolls sourced in Asia to lines like Fisher-Price's Little Mommy, which is a fully developed doll line. These dolls typically represent infants, and the play is all about nurturing, taking care of the doll and the child fantasizing about being the mommy to the doll. In addition to very basic dolls at a low cost, there are also lines like Corolle (owned by Mattel) that are more expensive, European-inspired dolls. Madame Alexander has in recent years expanded their offerings to include baby dolls, though the company is best known for its collectibles.

For the most part, adults are the ones buying dolls in this category, so they are often bought on the strength of in-store appeal and price point.

Traditionally, these dolls weren't licensed, but in recent years, Disney has introduced baby versions of the Disney Princesses, which include such characters as Cinderella or Ariel as babies. Regardless, the nurturing play is still the same. There have also been baby versions of popular lines like The Cabbage Patch dolls.

## Large Dolls

The prosaic name for this category is really a catchall for a variety of dolls. Established lines like Cabbage Patch Kidsfit under this, as do a multitude of other dolls that are based on popular licensed characters, but these can also be dolls that are very basic rag dolls as well. What distinguishes this category is that these dolls are about 12–20 inches tall, and they are basic playthings. This category has received a lot of attention in recent years thanks to Mattel's American Girl line that inspired a variety of different types of dolls with storylines designed to sell at a lower cost and sold through mass market retailers. Nickelodeon's Dora the Explorer has entries in this category, and in the feature doll sector as well. Disney has been very successful in this category with dolls produced by Jakks Pacific, encompassing Princess toddler dolls. LaLaLoopsy from MGA Entertainment, which combined a classic rag doll look with a contemporary plastic doll, drove sales in this category largely due to its unique look—and that it entered the market in 2010 when there wasn't that much competition in the category. In 2012, one of the hottest toys of the year was based on the Disney property Doc McStuffins, and in 2013 the newly launched Sofia the First, also from Disney, is changing this category, adding licensed, character dolls to a sector that was once dominated by generic baby dolls.

The play with these dolls is very narrative based, and whether it's a classic princess, a TV show or a story created for the doll, girls bring these dolls to life through imaginative play inspired by the stories.

Marketing for these dolls varies. Of course, where there's an entertainment property, that does a lot of the selling, but these dolls are also very advertising and promotion responsive, generally requested by the child rather than selected by the parent.

## Feature Dolls

These dolls share a lot of the characteristics with the large dolls, with the addition of some sort of active feature, usually electronic. These dolls dance, sing, eat, talk, and so forth. They, too, range from relatively simple dolls with a sound chip to more sophisticated, computer-powered dolls. They are mostly established brands, whether Hasbro's Baby Alive or dolls based on popular entertainment properties such as Dora the Explorer.

These dolls are, and need to be, widely television advertised. In fact, determining whether or not the doll will make a good commercial often features prominently in the product development process.

Marketers will often introduce a feature doll as a "key driver" for a large doll line. They have a higher price point, but may not deliver as strong a margin for the retailer as a basic doll in the same line. For example, a feature doll based on Dora the Explorer or LaLaLoopsy will be heavily TV advertised and can have an impact on driving awareness for the line overall.

The challenge with a feature doll is building enough play into it so that it becomes more than what is often called a "watch me toy," that is, a toy that goes through its paces but doesn't really require the interaction of the child. Concern about paying $50 or more for such toys (This has also happened in the plush category in recent years.) that don't foster interaction has prompted manufacturers to make simpler, less expensive toys. The sweet spot at retail for these toys is currently about $35–$39. Certainly in the seasons from 2010 on, dolls that are introduced at $60 or more sometimes languished on the shelves and started selling when the prices dropped. This is a compelling example in one product category, but it has relevance in the entire toy business. First, toys are very price sensitive, particularly as the competitive frame changes. Parents who were spending $80 and up for a doll now consider that level of expenditure in the context of a toy tablet or even as a contribution toward an iPad as something that they believe will provide longer term value for their children. Moreover, the swings of the industry can happen within the development cycle of a product. It took about 2 years for realizations and realities of a changed marketplace to show up in product that was already in the pipeline.

## Mini Dolls

This is another catchall category. Virtually any small, figural toy that is targeted to girls will be considered in this category. While the category was essentially created in the early 1980s with the introduction of Polly Pocket, a human character, today it encompasses cats, dogs, horses, fairies, aliens and a whole host of other types of creatures. In this category, it's the size that matters, and these are typically merchandised together.

Polly Pocket dominated the category for years and had relatively little competition, but while companies were competing in the larger doll categories around 2005 and 2006 when properties like "High School Musical" were competing heavily in the fashion doll category and taking all the business that wasn't going into Barbie or the Disney Princesses, the sleepy Mini Doll category became a hotbed of competition. Renewed marketing effort was put against classic properties like Hasbro's My Little Pony and Littlest Pet Shop, and the category became quite active again. At the same time, slight declines in Polly Pocket created a more open playing field, and, as happens in the toy industry, people rushed in.

Today, there are miniature versions of many of the popular large doll brands, such as LaLaLoopsy, and new entries are competing for space in the aisle. A mini doll can be a profitable addition to a franchise, but it is becoming more crowded.

Girls' play with mini dolls is more analogous to boys' play with action figures than to other types of doll play. The idea is to create a universe over which the girl has, not to be *too* dramatic, complete dominion. As a result, most mini dolls have some kind of playsets and themes that are developed every year. The advantage of this is that the playsets generally deliver a strong margin and provide an anchor for an individual girl's collecting and playing. Boys may be loyal to one line of action figures and buy deeply within it; the same goes for girls and mini dolls.

The diversity of the product in this category at this writing means that the barriers to entry are quite high. In addition to the costs of development and the challenges of getting retail placement, a competitive category requires significant investment in advertising and promotion; something many small companies may not be able to afford. Even large companies that have tried to get into this sector have ultimately not met expectations because more than ever, the story, characters and entertainment component are critical to establishing awareness and preference in the target audience.

The Mini Doll category is also facing another challenge that was previously unforeseen. The rise of girls' construction systems described earlier is a direct challenge to the mini doll. Barbie, for instance, does not have a typical mini doll, but the Barbie figures that are included in the Mega Bloks sets compete directly with other mini doll products. Thus, dollars that might have gone to this category are moving over to the building and construction category, another example of the shifting patterns of this business.

## Fashion Dolls

Put bluntly, it starts with Barbie and goes from there. This category has been dominated by the Girl from Malibu for many years, but it has also been a shifting category. Still, with the Barbie brand (including toys, lifestyle and all other Barbie-branded product) topping, approximately $3 Billion annually worldwide, she is the force to be reckoned with. As noted previously, Barbie's success has been in the ability to keep reinventing who she is in the context of the contemporary market. The genius, if you will, behind Barbie has been her very adaptability. She can take on different roles and personas while still remaining Barbie. She has been a lightning rod for controversy over the years (Who knew polyvinyl chloride was conductive?), but most of the controversy has happened over the heads of little girls. The same, too, happened with the legal wrangling between Mattel and MGA over the ownership of the Bratz property.

The dominance of Barbie notwithstanding, this has been a highly competitive category for the second-tier dolls, and it's getting even hotter. A boom in celebrity dolls, the introduction of the Disney Princess line, the challenge mounted by MGA with its Bratz and Moxie lines, has created a crowded category. There are new, themed doll lines from small companies that are making inroads into the business, and in the latter part of 2013, Barbie is facing new challenges in trying to stay relevant amidst the competition. Moreover, Barbie's world is generally white in a culture of growing ethnic diversity. However, no one is counting Barbie out yet. This is a brand that has consistently shown its ability to evolve in challenging markets, and you can bet that Mattel is not going to sit quietly by. Barbie's history, as noted earlier, is one of reinvention. One of the advantages Mattel also has is the ability to diversify its doll offerings, so while the Barbie brand will continue to develop, other intellectual property, such as Monster High, is filling the need for dolls both from consumer and revenue perspectives.

There is also one other significant advantage to the brand equity Barbie enjoys. Quite frankly, it's tough to put a new fashion doll concept into the market. Development and promotion costs are high, and getting retail support is not easy. For example, if a typical advertising-to-sales ratio is 5 to 10% in other categories (not always seen in the toy industry, incidentally), fashion dolls need to go big in order to break through to promotion responsive little girls. Warehouses are littered with dolls that might have been good concepts but lacked the promotion push to make them significant players.

Perhaps no single doll has reflected what it takes to be successful in this business in recent years than Mattel's Monster High. An internally developed property, it went from a standing start to approximately $1B in sales in 3 years on the market.

## Monster High: Scaring Up a Hit

An ability to read the market and translate that into a property that will resonate with girls is one of the strongest—and most consistent—assets of Mattel's doll group.

As Tim Kilpin, executive vice president and general manager of Mattel Global Brands, explains, as the doll team looked at the culture, they saw the fascination with novels like "Twilight," Goth fashion, and the supernatural impacting all aspects of the culture.

"You can't explain where the spark comes from," he says. "All you can do is create an environment where the spark happens. And who doesn't hate what happened in High School?"

But Mattel's thinking went more deeply. While an adult may look back at high school in embarrassment or dread, a girl in the core doll age looks ahead to high school as something to be romanticized. And so Mattel tested, and tested, and tested. Given a strong consumer response, the company was on a path to following a traditional toy strategy, but as the consumer response continued positive—and the culture didn't seem to grow tired of vampires and monsters with a youthful mien—the company realized that it had something bigger on its hands and decided to hold back until the characters could be more developed.

As Kilpin says, "the cost of failure is so high. You've got to do your homework." And so the storyline emerged of the teenage children of classic monsters. Draculaura is Dracula's daughter. Clawdeen Wolf is the daughter of the Wolfman and so forth.

Mattel also knew that to put this over with girls they needed to immerse them in the storyline. They produced webisodes for the characters, complete storylines, a universe for the dolls, all grounded in a reality that girls of the target age—initially 8–11—could relate to. Knowing, for example, that this is an age when kids are struggling to fit into their social context, each of the Monster High characters is an individual, has flaws they're sensitive about and still try to fit in. "Freaky is fabulous" became part of the story's positioning, and it was compelling and universal enough that girls related to it.

But it wasn't all smooth sailing. As Kilipin says, just before the launch Wal-Mart decided not to carry the doll, but Mattel was committed to it, and production was underway. And their insights were proven correct. The company had more than 1.5 million views of its video in the first weekend, and the ball started rolling. Incidentally, Wal-Mart has carried the doll with great success after recovering from its initial cold feet—and seeing the level of promotion that Mattel put behind the brand.

What Kilpin says in discussing the success of the brand, however, is that it all comes from consumer insight and understanding on an almost granular level what resonates with specific kids. A Monster High girl is not necessarily a Barbie girl, and determining the difference and being able to create characters that are relatable and aspirational opens up all kinds of opportunities.

One of the lessons of the success of Monster High is the understanding of how important story has become in launching fashion dolls. Ironically, when Ruth Handler launched Barbie in 1959, she was adamantly opposed to any kind of storyline being attached to Barbie. She felt that specific stories limited little girls' creativity, and they should be free to create any story they want. In 2013, stories are essential to attracting girls into a franchise. Far from being limiting, the stories become catalysts for girls to play out their own narratives and project them onto the characters.

Daunting as it may seem to try to enter the fashion doll market in the contemporary environment, there are still niches that are possible. Dolls based on entertainment properties or dolls targeting a specific and well-defined market can be profitable as long as the numbers are realistic. It's even possible that some of the me-too dolls that seek to capitalize on the trend of Monster High may make some money, but typically they do not fare very well. As in other industries, the first mover in a category very often becomes dominant, particularly when backed with significant marketing muscle.

The challenge is that while there may be opportunities for doll lines that make $20–$30 million in a year, the competition is fierce and the likelihood of being outspent and outflanked is tremendous, though for a small, aggressive company, a profit of $6 million on revenues of $30 can be considered a tremendous success.

Looking ahead, this will continue to be a category that is fashion-responsive and entertainment driven. As the monster themes mature, companies are looking for the next great theme and storyline to emerge. Certainly, the entire fashion doll sector has been looking for it. As you are reading this, the trend may have passed, but in mid-2013, one of the next emerging themes will be dolls with storylines based on the classic Fairy Tales. How well these are developed—and how effectively they're marketed—will determine the winners. Such tactics as webisodes, direct to DVD or digital movies, books, music, and other ancillary products are becoming central to this category. Although it may sound a little bit exaggerated, the challenge for any doll brand targeting the older end of this consumer spectrum (ages 6 and up) is to try to create a "lifestyle brand." That simply means offering many ways for kids to interact with the brand that go beyond the actual toy. On the one hand, this can be extremely expensive and time-consuming. On the other hand, compared to the expense of producing a TV show or movie, creating animation for the Internet and YouTube can be very inexpensive. That opens the door for start-up companies like S-K Victory, headed by industry veteran Ken Price, to compete at least in this arena with a company like Mattel. In some cases, the smaller companies may even have an advantage in that they can be more nimble and flexible in getting product and content into the marketplace. But then, and here we come back to square one again, it is about the product and the content, and what's going to appeal to the tastes of the young consumers.

Finally, as one looks at this category, it's important to understand it in the context of the typical play patterns of fashion dolls as a function of children's ages and cognitive development. Over the years, the age range for fashion doll play has dropped severely. While in the 1970s, it was common for girls as old as 10 or 11 to be playing with Barbie, in the contemporary market, the top age is often 8 (always excepting a phenomenon like Monster High that can extend the age with a novel concept that appeals to older girls). The age of entry into the market has also aged down with girls as young as 3 or 4 starting to play with fashion dolls. However, the way a 3-year-old and a 6-year-old relate to dolls are completely different based on their stage of cognitive development. As we'll see repeatedly, understanding the fine distinctions that happen in ages of children is essential to developing toys that will appeal to them.

When a fashion doll is a hit and lasts several seasons, there is also another phenomenon that generally happens and affects the line and the brand. This is known as "aging down." It occurs when younger girls see what older girls or older siblings are playing with and decide they want part of that, too. While this can broaden the market and offer new opportunities for sales, it also is an indication that the doll is approaching maturity in the marketplace. As younger children play with it, older children abandon it, and the doll and its storyline eventually have to become more accommodating of the younger demographic. Not that this is necessarily a bad thing: it fosters innovation and the development of new opportunities. This certainly has happened with Barbie, and in mid-2013, it has begun to happen with Monster High. Mattel, fully aware of this trend, has invested heavily in developing in new intellectual property to attract the consumers they may lose—as well as new ones.

The fashion doll category, in general terms, breaks down into three phases.

- Fantasy Play. These are the youngest girls for whom fairies, princesses, and other stories are the most compelling. This is usually in the 3–4 age range. Magic, fantasy and tons of glitter appeal to kids in this age group. These girls are very self-focused and only beginning to have cognizance of themselves in the context of the larger world.
- Grown-Up Play. Girls in the 4–5 age range begin to see themselves in the context of their world. The play replicates what they see in the home, replicating family relationships, and thinking about what they

want to be when they grow up. How else could Barbie have successfully had more than 130 careers?
- Teenage Play. As girls begin to be socialized outside the home at ages 5–6, they begin to fantasize about becoming teenagers, going to high school, and so forth. This is where Barbie play was in 1959, and it's still a part of girls' development. Rather than looking up to parents, girls start looking up to older girls, and the play is more fashion and friend related. This was the group that Bratz so successfully targeted by creating fashions that were reflective of what these girls were seeing in the world around them.

As with everything in the toy industry, these are not hard and fast rules. There are dolls like the Disney Princesses that cross over all three of these categories, but even if the dolls remain the same, the play will reflect the developmental stages.

## Collectible Dolls

As a category, collectible dolls are a minor contributor to the overall doll business and don't figure prominently in the mass-market toy industry, which is the primary focus of this book.

For the most part, collectible dolls are created by small, specialty companies and are sold through specialty stores, including FAO Schwarz, online and at doll shows. Doll collecting remains the second most popular hobby in the United States, and there are many small companies and artisans serving the collectors. At the same time, there are a handful of larger companies that serve this market segment, including the Barbie collector line, the famous Madame Alexander dolls, or the collection of artists' dolls sold by Ashton-Drake Galleries and other comparatively smaller concerns. Even the entertainer Marie Osmond has a line of dolls, which has proven to be extremely popular with collectors. The market, however, is predominantly adult women. It's a niche market. Madame Alexander's baby dolls and large dolls are considered in their respective categories.

However, in an attempt to broaden the doll market, several manufacturers have marketed dolls as collectibles. Largely targeted to girls and young women who are too old to play with dolls, but who may enjoy collecting and displaying them, versions of popular dolls from lines like MGA's Bratz, Mattel's Monster High and, of course, Barbie. Many of these include the so-called Limited Edition holiday dolls, though of course the limitation in many cases is based on the number of dolls that have been ordered.

Only Barbie, which has a robust and active fan base and collector community, has designed its collectible business in four tiers ranging from mass production to the Platinum tier in which only 1,000 dolls are made of a given variety.

In Mattel's case, the Pink tier, which has a potentially unlimited production run, is sold wherever Barbie is sold, but the rarer dolls are sold only online or at authorized specialty stores.

For a time in the mid-1990s, there was a perception that collectible dolls would significantly appreciate in value, based on record breaking sales for certain older collectibles. Adults bought dolls with the idea that they were investments. They were not, and today online auction sites are flooded with Barbie dolls, particularly, that are selling for not much more than their initial retail price, if that.

### *Dolls—What It Takes To Succeed*

It's impossible to create any kind of formula for success in such a diverse broad category. However, good product, strong promotion, and compelling storylines all contribute to potential, particularly in the fashion doll business.

Licenses for baby and large dolls can do well. In fashion dolls, these are limited keepsakes, and while a business can do well with a celebrity doll, for example, this is a quick in-and-out because the business will move on. After all, who would buy a Spice Girls doll today?

## Games and Puzzles

### *History*

Board games and puzzles have a long history. Chess, checkers, backgammon, and so forth have been around for centuries. Parcheesi created a sensation at the end of the beginning of the 20th Century, and Ouija Boards, Monopoly and many other classics began as fads. Many of the games introduced in the early years of the 20th Century are still made—Scrabble, Clue, Sorry, Candyland to name just a few.

In the 1960s, Marvin Glass introduced the skill-and-action game, and such classics as Mousetrap, Booby Trap, Ker-Plunk, Hands Down, and many more became hits with the Baby Boom generation. Othello followed in the 1970s, but shortly thereafter games stopped being played by adults, though kids games still sold, and by the early years of the 1980s, the conventional wisdom was that adults didn't play board games. (The one exception was Dungeons & Dragons introduced in the early 1970s that created the specialized niche of fantasy role-playing games that continues to have a strong following, as does Magic: The Gathering.)

The game business changed again with the introduction of Trivial Pursuit in 1983. Its success prompted many other companies to rush into the market with trivia games, most of which were too specialized and found a small market, if any. Adult games were back, and the launch of Pictionary in 1985 cemented that impression. Suddenly everyone was trying to create a game, and the lottery mentality that often infects the toy industry was pervasive. The New York Toy Fair during these years was full of games that people had taken second mortgages to produce, and many of them failed miserably.

During this time, even with the rise of video games, board games for kids continued to be a viable market. Hasbro acquired Milton Bradley in 1984 and Parker Brothers in 1987, securing its place as the largest game manufacturer. Western Publishing, which produced Pictionary, Pressman Toy, Cardinal, and other companies vied to get the game dollar, which was really an entertainment dollar for adults. During the economic downturn following the crash of 1987, it became popular to promote games as inexpensive home entertainment.

The fads of adult games passed, and while Pictionary and Trivial Pursuit continued to sell—and are still on the market in new and updated versions—the large, adult game market returned to its fairly stable performance. There was a burst of activity and popularity again in 1998 when Cranium was introduced, and the eponymous company had quite a run as it created award-winning games for kids of all ages. Hasbro acquired Cranium in 2008, and has not done much with the assets, allowing it to fade away.

Puzzles, on the other hand, have remained constant sellers. First introduced in the late 17th Century, these puzzles became mass-market sellers in the 1930s when new methods of cutting the puzzles were introduced. Puzzles have a devoted fan base that buys regularly, largely based on the photographs, and they continue to deliver high margins. Different configurations and even three-dimensional puzzles have been breakout hits in recent years, but this is generally a stable market.

## The Market Today

As noted, the puzzle market remains fairly stable. Companies like Ravensburger are introducing innovations, such as the ability for an iPad to scan a picture and activate a video. For the most part, though, puzzles are a solid, profitable business.

In 2013, the games market, however, is suffering. Several years of lackluster sales, the lack of any blockbusters and over-saturation of versions of Monopoly, Candyland, Uno and other classics have depressed sales. In 2012, physical versions of the Angry Birds app boosted game sales for Mattel and the category overall, but games based on other apps did not fare as well. Spin Master has emerged as a player in the category, but they have largely grown by acquiring products.

Indeed, while games can be relatively inexpensive to produce (often paper and ink with small plastic parts sourced, i.e., purchased rather than manufactured specifically for one game), the development of a good, playable game is highly complex. For companies like Spin Master, it's much more cost-effective to purchase independently produced games that have shown a track record in a limited market and give them broader distribution. Thus, the smaller specialty game stores and international markets have been proving grounds for games. The function of the larger game companies in many cases in the contemporary market is to serve as a distributor for a game that has already been vetted.

The larger companies have lagged in creativity in this category. In recent years, Hasbro and to a lesser degree Mattel have concentrated on trying to create new games based on established franchises. Thus, there have been a proliferation of games branded with Monopoly, Scrabble or

Uno. The strategy of managing game titles as if they were traditional brands has its challenges.

For example, Hasbro has continued to pump out a variety of games under its Monoply banner, just as Mattel has created many variations of Uno. The challenge is that consumers don't see a compelling reason to purchase a new game. In 2013, Hasbro launched a publicity stunt to replace the Iron from the traditional Monoply game with a new token that was voted on by consumers. While this got attention in the news, it did relatively little to spike Monopoly sales overall. Even Seth Meyers on "Saturday Night Live" joked, "The next time you play Monopoly, you can play as the iron because who is going to go out and buy a new game?"

The innovation is really coming from the smaller companies. A company like the Seattle-based Wonder Forge has been successful with a variety of preschool games, but as president Jacobe Chrisman notes, the success has to do with the combination of a good game and a strong license. They have successfully leveraged Dr. Seuss, Teenage Mutant Ninja Turtles, and Angelina Ballerina into profitable games. While the Wonder Forge invests heavily in game mechanics and gameplay, Chrisman also notes that getting retail placement without the licenses is virtually impossible. In a competitive field, the license has to sell the game, particularly when, with few exceptions, games don't generate the kind of revenue or margin that allow extensive television advertising for preschool and young children's games. (The skill-and-action games of the 1960s were heavily TV advertised, but that was a different world.) While Hasbro may invest against a brand like Monopoly or engage in an overall promotion for "Family Game Night," which incidentally had a positive effect on the entire games category.

Marketing for games, as it has since the mid-1980s, consists of publicity, promotion, and relatively lower cost tactics. Pictionary in the mid-1980s, famously sold more than one million games in approximately 18 months without any TV advertising and using only publicity and promotion at a time when sales of one hundred thousand units of a game was considered successful. Still, once a game has proven itself in the marketplace, TV advertising can be an effective tool for broadening that market. And, as we'll see in the coverage of the sell-in process later on, TV advertisement can figure into the mix. Still, the best way for games to grow is through word of mouth. People who enjoy games tend to want to share them with their friends. Disappointing games aren't played again, but that doesn't mean that it hasn't sold initially; it just means it won't be a blockbuster.

Ultimately, as we continue to see in every toy category, every game is different and every strategy is different. There are companies like Hasbro, Mattel, and Spin Master that will invest in TV advertising, while there are companies like Pressman and Cardinal that are less likely to.

### *Games & Puzzles—What It Takes to Succeed*

With puzzles, there are fairly low barriers to entry. A strong image, an innovative construction, or an added feature can be effective in attracting a consumer who is already predisposed to purchase puzzles.

No two games, on the other hand, are alike. There are so many variables in this category. For example, it's possible to sell a mediocre game with a strong license in the preschool aisle, as success is not necessarily measured by the pleasure a game provides the consumer but in its sales numbers. A strong property, such as Angry Birds, for instance, sells as much for its novelty appeal as the quality of its gameplay.

For manufacturers, a track record of profitable games is more likely to get placement at retailers than a new game. As noted earlier, that's where the specialty market comes in as a proving ground for games.

There are a few elements that characterize a good game, however. It must be easy to learn. People need to be able to open the box and be playing in very short order. (Always with the exception of games like Dungeons & Dragons where part of the playing experience is the set-up.)

It must be fun to play. As fundamental as that sounds, there are a lot of games that aren't fun. Turns take too long. It's complicated. Or, most importantly there's no social interaction. From a play standpoint, board games deliver an experience unlike any other in the toy industry. They are basically social experiences. Especially in the adult game category, but also in children's games, the interaction among the players that the game promotes must be as engaging as the game itself. Several years ago, Hasbro introduced versions of Monopoly and Battleship that had a computer module in the center. This dictated virtually every aspect of the gameplay, and it shut out the interaction among the players. Aside from the fact that it was very expensive, the game itself pre-empted the social experience.

This is also where the concept of game mechanics is critically important. How the game flows, how elements of chance and strategy are balanced and even down to the average length of the games all figure into whether or not it is viable once consumers get it home. Rigorous play testing and adjustments are required in the development process, but that doesn't always happen. It's expensive and time-consuming, which is what leads to some pretty boring, licensed preschool games especially. Still, if the game sells, the licensor gets its royalty and the manufacturer and retailer make money, that's the objective. This is anathema to real board game mavens and developers, but it is the reality.

The social experience also determines another important element: the game should be somewhat different each time it's played. Whether that comes from the different appearance of random elements or the different players, a game that is predictable and repetitive generally doesn't do well.

Good games can be a cash cow for years, or even decades. Yet of the hundreds of games people try to introduce each year, very few achieve that level of success. Thus, each game that a company decides to produce requires an individual marketing and sales strategy based on the variables of the market, the potential consumer, the projected life of the game, the experience of the gameplay and so forth.

In recent years, larger companies such as Mattel and Hasbro have attempted to take a branding approach to their games. That is, rather than invent wholly new games, they have taken established brands—Candyland, Monopoly, Uno and so forth, and tried to create line extensions that were essentially the same game but had a few new bells and whistles. While adding some revenue and helping to get a few more placements at retail, the consumers have been lukewarm on them. Why, for instance, buy another Candyland game when the price is significantly higher than the original, which is still sold, and there is no compelling reason for the consumer to trade up? In 2011 and 2012, Hasbro tried to group its word games under the Scrabble brand, but the result was confusion at the consumer level. What, consumers wondered, was Scrabble Boggle? In the consumers' minds these were two distinct brands and game experiences and combining them made no sense.

What all of this points up is that games are not like other sector of the toy industry. They have a wider potential audience in terms of age. With the exception of skill-and-action games that are very visual, they are hard to advertise on TV. They don't behave as a typical brand because even with new features, they're not consumable and can stay on the shelf for a long time, so it's hard to give a consumer a compelling reason to purchase.

However, having taken Hasbro to task a bit above, let's also give credit where credit is due. In 2013, the company relaunched several of its classic games—Pictionary, Taboo and Scattergories—in new, updated versions with faster gameplay and lower price points. Why does this have such strong potential? Well, for one, there is brand equity in all these names, but the changes acknowledge that in the last 20—25 years or so since these games were hits, the time people have to play games has diminished. Faster-playing versions of favorites is a strategy that leverages the brands and at the same time updates the game mechanics for a contemporary consumer/game player.

As for a formula that can be applied across the board? Forget it. In this way the game business is more analogous to the movie business than a consumer product business. Even when all the pieces are in place (to use a game pun), one never knows if something is going to be a success until the market weighs in.

## Pictionary—How a Hit Was Made

Though it's now nearly 30 years since it first drew attention, the story of Pictionary remains a model of how the game business can work, and certainly represents the dream that keeps people in their garages trying to come up with the hit. Of course, the realities of the business are that you have probably an equally good chance of writing a hit screenplay as coming up with a hit board game, but that doesn't stop people from trying.

Rob Angel came up with the concept of what was essentially charades on paper, and with $15,000 borrowed from family members, he assembled the first games in his apartment. His partners in the effort Terry Langston and Gary Everson handled the business end and design, respectively.

Unable to find a store that would carry the game, Angel set up a table in the Seattle flagship store of Nordstrom's and started playing the game and selling it to anyone who would stop by. The excitement was electric, and soon they were setting up game play in other Nordstrom stores, and the game sold out. Game companies were looking for the next Trivial Pursuit, and the unconventional sales technique came to the attention of Tom McGuire, an industry veteran who had been laid off from Selchow & Righter (makers of Scrabble and Trivial Pursuit). He had heard about this new game company looking for someone to handle sales. He did more than that; he created a whole new company initially of former Selchow sales reps called The Games Gang. Later they went into partnership with printer Joe Cornacchia and Western Publishing to be able to meet the demand. They hired noted publicist Linda Pezzano and her team (which included your author) in hopes that the Trivial Pursuit lightning would strike again. With a combination of game playing parties, grassroots marketing and getting a lot of people to play the game, within 2 years after the launch of the game, the team was celebrating the production of the one millionth game—at a time when selling 100,000 units in a year was considered a runaway success in the game business.

So, why is this relevant today? In the games sector, as we've seen a bit earlier, the major companies are not inventing in research and development. It falls to small companies—or individual inventors—to create games and demonstrate that there is a market for them. Then, a large company can either purchase the game outright or license it and provide a level of distribution and marketing that would be beyond the small company's capabilities.

The success of Pictionary points up one other essential component of effective game marketing: consumer trial. There is no other sector of the toy industry that is so responsive to trial and word-of-mouth in selling games. Getting those people most likely to purchase a game to try, purchase, share, and recommend it is an essential part of the process. Board games typically don't make good TV commercials, but good ones create entertaining experiences. Perhaps it's a little easier in today's market where blogs and online sites can facilitate word-of-mouth, but the principle remains unchanged.

## Infant and Preschool Toys

*History*

This is another dynamic category in the toy industry. Today, it encompasses all kinds of toys designed for children ages 3–6, though that's not a hard and fast rule. For tracking purposes, the definition of this category has been anything but constant. The category is also tracked to include infant toys as well as preschool toys, though the two are very different in terms of design and utility. The relatively new electronic learning toys were tracked separately from other non-electronic learning toys. Therefore, it can be maddening to attempt to construct any kind of coherent history of the category over time. One certainly can't get an accurate assessment of the changes in the growth of the category over any extended period because, as with other categories, advances such as electronics and the growth of licenses have reshaped and resized the category many times over the last 20 years.

There are, however, a few changes that have influenced the category today. In the 1990s and beyond many of the larger preschool brands such as Mattel's Fisher-Price and Hasbro's Playskool pulled out of the basics business. With the exception of licensed goods, generic rattles and teethers, stacking toys and so forth were being produced less expensively by many Asian companies and delivered better margins to retailers, and it became more and more difficult for major companies to compete in that sector. As a result, the larger companies began focusing on more and more sophisticated products using licenses. Sesame Street, Blues Clues, Dora the Explorer, Thomas the Tank Engine, SpongeBob, and so forth became staples of the business. (Sesame Street had been licensor whose products were marketed under the Child Guidance brand from the early 1970s, and it was rolled into the Playskool line when Hasbro acquired some of the assets of Child Guidance after the dissolution of CBS Toys in the mid-1980s.)

Preschool educational toys have also emerged over the last 20 years or so as a major contributor to this category. Starting in the mid-1980s, the electronic learning toy began to become a staple of the preschool business. Child Guidance was one of the first companies to have a major success in the category with its Talk 'N Play, which combined a book and a cassette tape to create an early reading experience. At the same time, Teddy Ruxpin was a huge hit using similar technology, though the bear itself appeared to read the story.

As computer chips began to be integrated into toys, VTECH pioneered the early electronic learning toys, and soon lights, sounds and rudimentary computer chips became basics in this business. In 1995, the preschool category was revolutionized with the Launch of LeapFrog and the subsequent introduction of the LeapPad became a huge hit.

All of this was played out against a cultural backdrop that emphasized early reading and the development of language skills. The entry requirements for kindergarten had become more achievement focused in terms of pre-reading, and parents were turning to LeapPad and toys that helped children with phonics as essential tools. At the same time, there were studies that suggested that listening to classical music improved children's ability to learn, and an entire line of Baby Einstein toys was born. (The study has since been debunked, but not before the company sold millions of pieces and was acquired by Disney.)

During these years toy companies capitalized on the fashion for early learning, and though the toys were excellent and, certainly in the case of LeapFrog, pedagogically sound, it's another indication of how cultural fashions drive the business.

## *The Market Today*

The preschool business in 2013 is crowded and competitive. At the major companies, licensing predominates, whether in stand-alone toys or as content for educational toys. The licenses more than the manufacturers are what consumers are shopping for. Yet there are variations within this. Under age 2, parents are usually making the purchase decisions, embracing Sesame Street and Winnie the Pooh, for example. However, once a child hits age 2, he or she becomes the specifier, asking for toys based on Thomas the Tank Engine, Dora the Explorer, Disney's Cars and so forth, based on what he or she is watching on TV. Newer properties such as Doc McStuffins, Sophia the First and Jake and the Neverland Pirates from Disney have shaken up the business, taking sales from some of the more established properties as new children discover these. The preschool licensing business can be highly volatile, requiring significant investment in tooling and design and a lead-time of about 18 months to get toys into the marketplace, making a licensing commitment both necessary and somewhat risky in a changing world.

While there is still lead time and investment in licenses, companies like VTECH and LeapFrog are creating software to go with their established, electronic learning platforms. Reflecting the development of technology in the adult world, particularly the rise of tablet computers, both VTECH and LeapFrog have introduced preschool tablets. These have included proprietary content, learning and entertainment software featuring licensed characters, all of which been critical to their success.

Companies like Fisher-Price are also once again trying to get into the preschool basics business and are developing sub-brands to differentiate product in the market. Fisher-Price's Little People and Imaginext brands attract older preschoolers, the latter using licenses like Batman re-imagined for a 4-year-old and their own characters, and Laugh 'N Learn, one of several homegrown sub-brands. Still, these brands face intense competition on price and quality for what are essentially basic toys. While in the 1960s and 1970s, the Fisher-Price brand had a great deal of equity in the preschool basics category, they have not been able to recapture that in 2013.

In the contemporary market, there is another factor that is impacting sales. Tablets and apps have changed the competitive frame in the preschool market. As noted above, both VTECH and LeapFrog have introduced toy-like tablets designed for the exclusive use of preschoolers; preschool apps on adult tablets are competing with some traditional toys. The iPad and Android tablets that adults use are easy to load up with apps and entertainment for kids, particularly on the go. Moreover, there are several competing companies that have introduced Android tablets that have dedicated apps and software, as well as parental controls, that allow an adult tablet to be used by children in what is considered safe for them—i.e., they have limited access to internet or anything not deemed appropriate for children. In 2013, these tablets range in price from about $60 to $200 and although parents do want to limit the amount of screen time kids engage in (TV, computer, tablet, Smartphone, etc.), these are competing for dollars that previously might have gone into traditional toys. Traditional toy manufacturers have responded by trying to create toys that leverage the technology and integrate it with a plastic toy. As of this writing, none of these has been a breakout hit, primarily because children's app time is often when parents are on the go, and they don't want to be burdened with a great deal of extra stuff to carry. Moreover, the apps themselves need to be engaging for kids, and few companies have the expertise or the ability to invest in the app development.

One other, perhaps unforeseen, impact of the boom in technology has been to make the preschool category more price sensitive. With a LeapFrog LeapPad costing about $100, parents have looked twice at spending $70 for interactive plush that, to their mind, does significantly less. This has caused companies to go back and look at their pricing and product development.

Even as the mass-market preschool business continues to be dominated by licensed products and technology, there are still niche markets. Much has been said in recent years about the growth of "green" toys for this sector. There are companies that do sell toys made of biodegradable plastic or natural fibers or made of wood from sustainable sources. While catering to an affluent and small demographic group, these toys may be profitable for the companies who produce them, but they do not figure significantly in the overall preschool marketplace.

## *Preschool Toys—What It Takes to Succeed*

For the mass-market preschool business, there really are three subcategories: educational, licensed and basics.

Parents and caregivers are the primary purchasers of educational toys, especially for younger kids, and these products need to be marketed on the basis of educational outcomes. At this writing, that focus is on pre-reading and early numbers competency.

The licensed sector depends largely on the license and its popularity. Understanding the properties and how kids interact with them and how they want to reflect that in their play is crucial to success in this category. TV advertising and other forms of promotion are critical, but the power of the property to appeal to kids is also a key factor. It's also critical to understand the competitive nature of these properties and who the purchaser is. For example, while both boys and girls will watch Dora the Explorer on TV, girls are the primary consumers of product based on the character, though there is a market for boys with the Diego character. Understanding the nuances of a license and the ways in which kids play with the characters is essential to developing engaging toys.

Case in point: The children's show "Dragon Tales" was a very successful, award-winning show that ran on PBS from 1999 to 2005. The toys based on the show did not perform up to expectations. Part of this was the competitive frame; it was the heyday of the Teletubbies and Blue's Clues to name just two other properties in the market at the time. Hasbro was producing both the Teletubbies and the Dragon Tales toys, and with few exceptions produced stuffed toys based on the characters. What was missing was the central element of the show—the Dragon Scale, which allowed the human characters to be transported into the world of Dragon Tales. Our interviews with kids at the time found that fans of the show were making their own and creating their own adventures. This piece was critical to the play, yet neither the licensee nor the licensor thought to produce it.

The final consideration for this is that while kids will watch a great number of shows, the ones they want to play are much more limited. A realistic understanding of the size of the potential market for these toys is essential—and it changes as shows come and go.

The challenge in the basic end of the business is to create a compelling story for a given product or product line. The case for sub-brands is that no single product is going to generate the kind of revenue that will justify significant investment in marketing and advertising, but aggregated across a sub-brand, these products, which can be promotion responsive, have a better shot at finding an audience.

## Outdoor and Sports Toys

### History

This category encompasses everything from playground balls to Frisbees to sandboxes. Basically, if it's going to be played with outdoors, it fits into this category. Almost as long as there have been human beings, there have been balls and other outdoor toys. Archaeologists found yo-yos and jacks when the pyramids were opened, and boomerangs, clackers and other classic toys were initially weapons used in hunting.

Given the breadth of products that fall under this heading, it's virtually impossible to make generalizations about this category, or even forecast performance. There are staple brands like Frisbee or Wiffle Balls. Little Tikes is known for its molded sandboxes, Furnise for bubble toys. This can also include Hasbro's NERF and Super Soaker lines, which one can't possibly compare to a generic playground ball in terms of performances, market responsiveness or brand impact.

## *The Market Today*

Despite the diversity of product, there are several significant factors about this market segment. First, it represents about 10% of the total United States toy market, much of which is divided among comparatively small companies once you take out major brands like NERF. Second, while the majority of toy sales are concentrated in the fourth quarter, the bulk of these sales come in the spring and summer, from the end of April through July 4.

As to what distinguishes toys in this category, it has largely to do with the product and what buyer is assigned to it at the various retailers and where the product is merchandised in the store. (Incidentally, this is not always consistent from store to store.) Finally, with a few exceptions, these toys are not heavily marketed, which allows them to deliver fairly high margins to retailers.

## *Sports and Outdoor—What It Takes To Succeed*

There are branded products, like NERF, Wiffle Ball, Frisbee and so forth, and there are commodity products. Each is going to perform differently. While Hasbro puts significant marketing dollars behind its NERF brand, a basics company does not. As a result, there are no rules or formulas that can be applied across the board to try to create any kind of commonality across this category.

However, that said, there are opportunities in this category. Take, for example, a relatively new company called Zing. They make foam arrows, slingshots and shooting toys of all types. Focusing on high performances and active play, they have made serious inroads into the category in just a few years. They have taken classic play patterns that parents might object to (a slingshot or bow and arrow, for instance) and made them safe, fun and satisfying to play with. Getting the "wow" factor into the toys has helped them distinguish themselves in the market.

## Plush—AKA Stuffed Animals

### History

This category traces its modern history to 1903 when the Ideal toy company created the Teddy Bear, based on a legend that Teddy Roosevelt had refused to shoot a baby bear cub on a hunting trip in Mississippi. The incident was made famous by a political cartoon in the Washington Post, and Morris Michtom created a toy out of "Teddy's bear," and getting permission from Roosevelt to use his name, the Teddy Bear entered the culture. (To be fair, the Steiff company in Germany had been making stuffed toys for about 20 years at the time of this incident.) The same year, the first licensed plush toys were introduced—based on Beatrix Potter's "Peter Rabbit." A decade or so later, Raggedy Ann and Andy became popular toys, and there were stuffed toys made of many popular characters, many now obscure including The Yellow Kid and Mutt and Jeff.

Traditionally, there have been basic plush toys and licensed plush toys. Companies such as Steiff, Gund and, more recently, Ty and Aurora have become major brands in the category, known for basic plush toys. Ty, of course, is famous for the Beanie Babies fad from the mid-1990s.

Licensed plush toys have been made by the holders of the licenses based on virtually every kids' property over the years. Care Bears, Teletubbies, Disney characters and countless others have been highly profitable for their manufacturers.

The mid-1990s saw the rise of electronic or feature plush. The legendary Tickle Me Elmo was introduced in 1996. Furby followed in 1998, and Zhu Zhu Pets in 2009 each were runaway fads and inspired all kinds of imitators and annual introductions as companies tried to answer the question, "What's the next Tickle Me Elmo?"

In 2005, Ganz introduced its Webkinz line of plush, small toys that had codes on the tags that kids could enter to get access to an online world, touching off another rush to have toys that integrated in some fashion with the web.

## The Market Today

Merely looking at the numbers, the plush market appears to be highly volatile, dropping 21% between 2010 and 2011. Dramatic as that figure is, however, much of that loss can be attributed to the fall off in Cepia's Zhu Zhu Pets, which had inflated the category in 2010, a fall off in feature plush and a lack of a hot property in the plush category. When those variables are removed we see, as we often do, that the category has remained relatively flat over the past 10 years.

Licensing continues to make a major contribution to the category, with new licenses Skylanders from the Activision video game existing side-by-side with classics like Care Bears and basics. Hasbro's Furreal Friends line has continued to perform well, marrying classic pet play with animatronics. In 2012, Hasbro relaunched Furby, and while it didn't approach the 40-million plus pieces the original sold, it was one of the best-selling toys of the 2012 holiday season.

Pricing continues to be a challenge in the feature plush aisle. In the years since Tickle Me Elmo laughed all the way to the bank, manufacturers created more and more complex and feature-driven items. Elmo did the Chicken Dance, Hokey Pokey and got increasingly more complex. In 2006, Hasbro introduced a $300 plush pony that was about the size of a real Shetland Pony. After Fisher-Price lost the Sesame Street license to Hasbro in 2009, the company created elaborate Rock Star Mickey, while Hasbro introduced a $70 Elmo, which when all the accessories were purchased cost more than $125. Prices got beyond what the market would bear, and there was a consumer backlash against what were considered to be "watch me" toys—toys that went through their paces and didn't require the interaction of the child. The category was getting bloated, and parents were looking at the growing prices and saying no, or at least waiting until the prices came down. Retailers were quick to mark down the items, and once they dropped below $50, they started to sell. There is still a market for so-called feature plush, but it is increasingly price sensitive, and manufacturers are finding that fewer bells and whistles are actually enough to deliver a solid play experience for the child.

Plush toys are comparatively inexpensive to manufacture and the lead times on them are shorter than molded plastic toys. It's easier to get plush toys into the market when a license gets hot, for instance, than a figure or a playset. For the most part, they are not TV advertised, but one of the rationales for the expensive toys described above was that these toys could be TV advertised, and the promotion would have a halo effect on the entire brand. In fact, product development has often been dictated by the need for a product to make a compelling TV commercial. The addition of the shaking to the original design for Tickle Me Elmo was specifically done to give the toy motion that would play well on a TV commercial.

Retail outlets for licensed plush are mostly the mass market, while generic plush toys are sold in specialty stores as well. Given that these are not always purchased for children, they are sold in a wide variety of gift shops, florists, chain drug stores, and so forth.

There is also a significant market for plush toys in the amusement category. These are usually tracked separately from the mainstream toy industry, but these include items created specifically for theme parks, game machines, and other non-traditional retail environments.

### *Plush—What It Takes to Succeed*

For licensed plush, a strong license is absolutely essential. Even that isn't a guarantee that a line will be successful across the board. Producing a line in different sizes and with different features can broaden the potential for distribution. A drug store, for instance, make take a small item while mass merchants will sell larger ones.

For basic plus, outside the known brands mentioned above—Steiff, Gund, Ty, Aurora—retailers buy based on price and margin and the appeal of a product. These are the same criteria consumers use, by the way.

## Vehicles

### *History*

It should come as no surprise that toy cars have been around as long as real cars have been. The romance of the automobile when it was new completely captivated the culture—and it has continued to do so for nearly a century. Wooden cars, metal cars and later plastic cars brought the sense of freedom to kids and allowed collectors to dream of owning an expensive car, or revisiting the classics of a bygone era. In the middle of the 20th Century, Corgi created miniature replicas of favorites, leveraging advances in manufacturing technology to make better and better models. In 1952, Matchbox was launched and soon became a dominant toy car company, specializing in 1:46 scale toys and costing about 99 cents. In the late 1950s, advances in battery technology made powered toy cars possible, and rudimentary (i.e. tethered) remote control vehicles. Throughout the 1950s and into the 1970s, America's love affair with cars grew and grew. The unveiling of new models was big news, and going to dealerships to see new models was a popular pastime. In 1968, vehicle toys got an injection of energy as Mattel unveiled its Hot Wheels line, and a whole new generation of kids was captivated. Hot Wheels added tracks and racing to the play, and quickly became established as a leading boys' brand.

One can't talk about this market without mentioning Tonka. First introduced in 1947, Tonka has been a mainstay of the vehicle business for more than 60 years. The classic construction vehicles and rescue themes have been part of preschool play for more than 60 years.

But this category was—and is—much more than just scale models and replicas. Advances in remote and later radio control opened up new opportunities and markets. The category also came to include licensed toys (The Batmobile, for instance), and as NASCAR continued to grow in the adult world, there was a concurrent boom in branded toys. Monster Trucks figured in the mix as well.

"Vehicles" doesn't just refer to automobiles. The category includes toy versions of anything that's motorized and moves. Airplanes, helicopters, fantasy vehicles and more are all considered in this broad category.

Like the other sectors that we've discussed, the business has remained fairly constant in terms of its size, at about $1.6 billion. In the middle of the 2000s, there was a boom in the category, occasioned by several concurrent factors: a boom in NASCAR, the popularity of miniaturized radio control vehicles, a boom interest in die-cast collecting and the popularity of Hasbro's Transformers (though not all these toys are tracked in this category), surrounding the opening of the first two movies. Ultimately, these ran their courses, and the market returned to its historic sales pattern, demonstrating once again the impact of the individual product on the overall category.

## The Market Today

Like every other category that we've been discussing, the vehicle category comprises many different products and different consumers. Like dolls that have an adult collector component, there is a portion of the vehicle segment that appeals to adults, whether as collectors or in the higher end radio control vehicles. So, let's look at these individual segments.

The basic, die-cast vehicles business is in flux in 2013. Cultural changes have affected the Hot Wheels business. It's still the largest selling toy brand in the United States based on unit sales, but the fascination with cars that was so pervasive in the culture in the 1960s, 1970s and, to some extent, the 1980s has passed. Mattel has put a lot of focus on track sets, different play patterns and has invested in entertainment. The challenge is to maintain viability in the market, particularly in changing competitive environment where vehicle play has to compete with action figure play and entertainment for boys' attention. What we've seen in this category has been a compression of the core ages, and with some exceptions, kids have given up these vehicles by age 6. As a result, Mattel has leveraged the Hot Wheels brand into a variety of products that are not, strictly speaking, vehicles including a line of stunt tops. (Mattel's Wizzzers stunt tops in 1970 were one of the hits of the year, another classic play pattern.)

Other basics, including the Tonka line, have stayed strong within the sector, building on the heritage of the brand. Hasbro, which owns the Tonka line, has licensed it to Funrise, a small, nimble California-based company that has produced a strong line of basic trucks that can be sold at a very attractive price point. These are the kind of toys that can deliver high margin to the retailers and an attractive price to consumers, building on the heritage of the Tonka brand, which resonates with parents and grandparents, important players in the toy-buying world. There are also a variety of other manufacturers producing basics in what is a very price-sensitive category.

Vehicles based on entertainment properties will change based on the movies and TV shows in a given year. Transformers remains a staple brand, with sales fluctuating in movie and non-movie years. Broad-based licensing programs for movies and TV are often tracked by the property, but for some movies there are some that have more vehicles than others—and, to throw another wrench into this—there are vehicle toys that are considered playsets. Again underscoring how difficult it is to get a consistent read on the category. In the current market, the NASCAR license, though still popular as entertainment, has fallen off in popularity among kids.

The radio control (R/C) segment is equally diverse. If there has been one trend in recent years, it has been the growth of miniaturized, flying R/C. Spin Master's Air Hogs brand is currently the leader in the flying R/C sector. Innovations in technology have made smaller toys possible with better performance and a better user experience almost every year, all while keeping the prices comparatively low. Prior to these innovations, most flying R/C planes and helicopters were considered hobby grade and very expensive. Spin Master brought the price down and allowed indoor flying, which has been a competitive advantage.

R/C cars run the gamut from simple preschool vehicles (often tracked in preschool toys or in an entertainment category) to more complex vehicles of many different sizes.

The recent trend toward operating the cars with an app from a Smartphone or tablet, while creating a flurry of interest and media attention, has ultimately proven less successful. In 2013, many companies have also included traditional R/C controllers with app-enabled toys to broaden the toy market. The level of investment required to create an effective app has also added to cost while not providing an offsetting competitive advantage in appeal to consumers.

## All Other Toys

Yes, that's really a tracked category in the toy business. At about $1.3 Billion, it's about 5% of the business, and it encompasses thousands of individual toys not covered by any of the supercategories. Walk through a toy store, and you'll see these toys that include promotional items, impulse items, bubble toys, accessories and so much more.

This category is as big as action figures, plush and close to the size of vehicles and building sets. It can be frustrating to a student of the industry, and it underscores both how different this business is from other industries and the importance of the individual product.

After all, it's from this category that Silly Bands came. And, yes, those were animal-shaped rubber bands that were hugely popular and made a fortune. Could anyone have predicted that? Absolutely not. And since when is a rubber band a toy? That's what keeps people in this business—and potentially drives them crazy or makes them very rich...or both.

# CHAPTER 3

# Product Still Rules

Talk to any retailer, any manufacturer—or kid for that matter—and you'll hear versions of one thing: it all comes down to the individual product. While it's important to understand the supercategories covered in the previous chapter in order to have a grasp of the industry overall, it's also obvious that there are many variations between products within a category. Just take Vehicles, for instance, the category encompasses items that cost less than a dollar and several hundred. Yet what all successful toys have in common is that they deliver fun, and they deliver it to a sufficient number of people so that manufacturers and retailers can make a profit by it. In this chapter, we'll take a look at the process by which products come to market.

Products may vary wildly, but the process of getting a product from an idea to a store shelf is fairly similar, whether it's done by a major, publicly traded corporation or a couple of guys in the garage. The former may have formalized procedures and the latter may be more of a bootstrap operation, but the objective for both is identical. A company must produce a product that can be made and marketed for a cost that retailers will stock and consumers will buy. In that way, the toy industry is identical to any other manufacturing business.

But it wouldn't be the toy industry if there weren't some idiosyncratic twists and turns along the way. After all, the decision as to whether the product you or your company has invested time and money in is viable is often in the hands of a 6-year-old child. These are not adult consumers making rational decisions. This is almost completely unbridled id desiring something in the heat of the moment. Whereas most marketing can tout the features and benefits of a product, virtually all sales to children are based on emotion. (Sales to adults are often done on emotion, too, but there are usually left brain rationales for the decision, something that doesn't happen with kids.)

So, let's take a look at how a product gets from the drawing board to production. (We'll talk about how it gets into the store and consumers hands subsequently.)

## The Nature of the (Sometimes Cuddly Plush) Beast

As noted above, somewhat flippantly but accurately, toys and games are consumed by the youngest consumers, and as such are constantly changing. That requires a level of constant reinvention that one doesn't see in a traditional consumer products company. A company that makes toothpaste or detergent can add newness by changing the formula, adding a bit of sparkle, something that the company can hang a marketing campaign on and get consumers to try. You can add an extra blade to a razor cartridge, but it's still a razor. You know your customer is going to buy razors; you just have to make yours more attractive and give consumers a reason to try. Toys, on the other hand, are a completely discretionary purchase. No one *needs* to buy toys. The final purchase decisions have to do not with utility but with emotional gratification—whether it's the giver or the receiver. Children grew and developed and became productive members of their societies for millennia before the advent of the contemporary toy business. Our cultural beliefs and traditions have created the perceived need for playthings. So to be completely blunt, the challenge is to come up with something no one needs and create a market for it and sell enough of it so that you can do it again—next year. Remember, we said earlier that approximately 40% of the toys on the shelves are new every year.

## Concept

Every toy starts with a concept, an idea. This can be a brainstorm; it can be a brand extension. It can be internally developed or bought from an inventor. It can be a sketch on a napkin or a fully developed sketch. The objective at this point in the process is to be able to communicate the idea and begin the process of determining viability while keeping costs as low as possible.

For the most part this stage will consist of sketches, write-ups and so forth. The idea is to try to get enough down on paper so you can move to the next stage. At the same time, you'll want to think through the play experience, whether this is a one-off product or one toy in an entire line. Should it be merchandised within a brand?

And, even though we've mentioned earlier that at the end of the day no one really needs toys, you need to consider what perceived need will it fill, or what entertainment value will it deliver.

In the case of a licensed property based on a TV show or movie, you'll want to consider how the play experience complements the entertainment and can be delivered in a way that kids will want to play.

Finally, while it's still in the early stages, you'll want to consider the retail price and where that will fall relative to the average for similar and competitive toys.

## Internal Development versus Working with Inventors

Research and development are expensive and time-consuming, and the results are not guaranteed. While major companies do have teams who work on product development, very often toy companies will turn to the inventor community for concepts. This does not mean that ideas are not developed internally at companies and the ratio to internally developed products versus those created by inventors varies widely by company, category and brand.

Most of the major toy companies have internal organizations whose job is to work with inventors, review concepts and make recommendations for how an idea can be developed.

A manufacturer's inventor group may, for example, put out a call that they are looking for a product in a certain category for a certain age group. Inventors present concepts and ideas, and potentially one is either bought, or more often, licensed.

Essentially, the manufacturer can outsource the concept development. However, the manufacturer will be intimately involved in the process of refining the product and tailoring it to their needs and determining production feasibility and so forth.

Perhaps one of the most famous examples of how an outside invention can be transformed into a hit is Tickle Me Elmo. When the product people from Tyco first saw the product, it was a monkey that giggled when it was hugged. Tyco, which at the time held the license for Sesame Street toys, felt that it would work as an Elmo character, since Elmo was known for its laugh and Tyco needed a lead item for the line. Later, the advertising agency suggested the vibration since the toy needed some visual hook for a TV commercial as well.

Every deal is different. Some inventors work on a royalty basis, with royalties varying from 5 to 7%, while others sell the concepts outright. As always, it depends on the toy and the situation.

Inventors specialize in specific product categories as well, and a couple of hits can make an inventor very wealthy, though many ideas never see the light of day. It's a risky business, but an integral part of how one aspect of the contemporary toy business works.

## Validation

If there is one stage of the process that too often gets short shrift, particularly among independent inventors but also within large toy companies, it's this one. And it's the one that can be the most critical in determining the viability of a toy.

Sure, you have a great idea. Your mother loves it. Your friends think it's cool. It's on strategy for a line extension, in the case of a large company. And very often that's all the validation people seek before starting to produce a toy. This is particularly true in the board game sector, where comparatively low production costs make it easy to get in.

But it's not just the "little guys" who make this mistake. What seems like a good idea may not be when all things are considered, and toys that are not sufficiently validated often end up failing. While there will be times for research and re-validation up to a certain point throughout the production process, this early stage is critical.

The first thing you'll have to do once you have your concept is consider the market. Who is this for? What is the age group? Does it fit into an established category? Does it fit into an established brand or product line? What does the competitive marketplace look like?

Defining your market is critical. The toy market is so diverse and so fragmented that having realistic assessment of the potential for a toy will determine the majority of the next steps you make.

The biggest mistake made at this stage is in targeting an age group that is too broad. While attaching a broad age to a toy appears to broaden the market potential, in actuality, toys have a very short life with the end consumer. Six months to a year is a very long time in the life of a child. Still, children develop at different paces, so a toy that some children have outgrown at five, others may find appropriate. The objective at this stage is to find the realistic "sweet spot." A toy may potentially appeal to kids from 3 to 6 years old, for example, but the age at which the majority of your sales are going to be made may be 4 to 5. This is where understanding children's cognitive and physical development is critical. You can always put a broader age range on the package to accommodate variations, but knowing where the largest part of your potential market is key to later stages of development.

Fitting into an established category is not absolutely required, but it can be very helpful if you're trying to sell into a retailer. They want to know where in the story to put it, for starters. In the current market, we're seeing some level of flux in this stage of the process. And all retailers won't always agree with your assessment. Wal-Mart may carry something in one aisle and Target in another and Toys "R" Us in yet another. Different buyers also cover different categories. At this stage of the process, however, you'll want to know where your product fits in the industry as a whole, or begin the process of looking at alternative ways the product can be merchandised. (These will be discussed in the chapter on retailing.)

When you consider the competitive field, it's important to look beyond just the toys that are directly competitive and to consider the entire range of toys that make up a child's entertainment at any given time. Thus, a doll can be competitive with an arts and crafts set or an action figure is competitive with a game, a vehicle or even a computer. Moreover, it's important to figure out what you're going to bump off the retail shelf or out of a kid's toy box to drive your sales. Kids' tastes and wants change rapidly, but at the same time, you have to realize that before retailers or kids pick something up, they have to put something down.

Part of looking at the competitive market is also to identify holes in the marketplace, under-merchandised areas that present opportunities. This may seem like a no-brainer, but consider that in a year when the fashion dolls sector, the opportunity for new entries may be fewer and the barriers to entry higher in terms of advertising and marketing costs to drive a product into a tight and competitive market.

It also bears repeating that, as discussed in the previous chapter, a central component to knowing where your toy is going to fit in the market and in the retail mix is to identify what you're going to knock off the shelf. For a retailer to take a new product, another one has to go. Even with the nearly 40% turnover of products in a given year, toymakers need to be able to articulate a strategy around a product introduction, such as understanding where a competitive product is in its life cycle and being able to market effectively against that.

As we've seen repeatedly, however, there is an exception for every premise and practice. The foregoing assumes that your concept is something new. There is also a huge market in the toy industry for so-called me too product. In this case, similar products are deliberately launched into the marketplace to take advantage of momentum in a category and pick up a different, more price-sensitive sector of the market. Retailers may, in fact, request a company to come up with something similar in a category to drive competition and potentially deliver a higher margin. (This is not something that many toy companies are willing to discuss or that makes them very happy, as you might imagine.) Trademark, copyright, patent, and trade dress protections are very strong in the United States, so one isn't likely to see the "Babie" [sic] doll sold in the United States, but until it was successfully shut down, it was seen in various international markets.

## Prototypes

So, let's assume that you've done your homework, and your concept has survived the scrutiny and it's gone through thus far. The next stage is usually to build prototypes. If you are making a simple toy, you may only have a prototype that looks like what you envision the finished product to be—at that time. However, most toys will have two kinds of prototypes, particularly if there is some kind of mechanism in the toy. Generally, the designers and engineers create "looks like" and "works like" models.

The names are pretty self-explanatory. The looks like model may be hand sculpted, the works like may be simply a mechanism at this stage and is really designed to see if the movement and performance of the concept is possible.

What follows are several rounds of development as the products are refined. At each stage, different elements are added as materials and components are selected for the finished product. At some point the two models merge, and what you have is what is typically called a "hand sample," a version that closely approximates the finished toy, but is a one-of-a-kind, hand-built model.

It's also during the prototype process that engineers begin to determine the cost of production. Assuming you've set your target retail price in the earliest stages of development, the challenge becomes determining if the concept can be executed within that cost range. Part of the costing includes making the margin. While margins can vary within the industry and between categories based on whether or not something is TV advertised, a good rule of thumb in the current market is to consider between a 30 and 35% margin on a toy.

Let's look hypothetically, and in round numbers, at how that could work for a toy that you need to be able to retail for $30.

- To make a 30% margin, the retailer needs to be able to purchase that toy for $21.
- Ideally, the manufacturer can produce the toy for about $11.
- That $11 unit cost has to include the product, packaging, shipping, advertising, licensing fees (if relevant), and all costs related to the production.
- It will vary by product, but that means that the product component of that may be 50% or less, so the product needs to be produced for maximum of $5.50, including materials and labor.

So, the challenge at the prototype stage is to figure out if the product can feasibly be produced within the targeted structure. Very often, the materials are the least expensive part of the toy. Reducing costs, however, is a paramount concern, and the equation is fragile. In recent years, the increased costs of shipping, materials, labor, and even electricity in China have had an upward pressure on production costs, even as retailers have exerted downward pressure on pricing. Add to this that a toy may only have a single year in which to recoup its investment and turn a profit, and the challenge becomes even greater. What this means is that each toy must be addressed as a stand-alone endeavor, and so the prototyping process is all about trying to ensure that the toy is feasible within the cost parameters. This is true whether a toy is to be manufactured in a factory owned by a toy company (comparatively rare) or if it is being sent out to bid by different factories.

The costing process can often set off internal conflicts, as the initial concept may appear to be too expensive to produce anywhere close to the targeted retail price, and so the process of cost reduction begins. Yet again, toys are somewhat unique compared to other manufactured goods. Many products can be successfully cost-reduced without harming function. However, the risk in the toy industry is that in reducing costs, one also reduces play features, and it's possible to end up with a toy that can be produced for a target cost but that doesn't deliver the play experience.

Prototypes also play a role in the sales process. While a retailer may have seen concept boards and presentations on a prospective product, the prototype stage is usually the point at which a retailer sees a version of what will eventually appear in store. While works like/looks like prototypes are expensive to produce, costing thousands to tens of thousands of dollars, the retailer feedback is critical at this stage and part of the ongoing dialogue between the retailer and the manufacturer.

## Production and Testing

Assuming a toy can be produced at a target price point and that retailers have ordered it, the toy then goes into production. Depending on the toy, production can be everything from molding plastic to cutting and sewing fabric to printing. The manufacturing processes for toys are not much different than those for other consumer goods. Our purpose here is not to discuss basic manufacturing processes, but to highlight what one needs to consider about the toy industry as distinct from other manufacturing operations.

Because children play with toys, and because most children under 3 year old will put things in their mouths, safety standards for toys are very strict. The U.S. Consumer Products Safety Commission and ASTM.org list the various requirements for materials and testing.

In addition to tests for shipping feasibility, toys undergo tests such as bite tests, drop tests, pull tests for buttons and strings, and other tests designed to simulate foreseeable use of a toy.

Recent scares such as lead in paint or the impact of strong magnets being ingested have created heightened public attention to toy safety. In response, companies have heightened oversight and increased testing at different stages of manufacturing. For example, in some cases where paints were tested only when the toy was produced, now paints are being tested before production begins before they've been applied to the toys and again when the toy is finished.

At the same time, in addition to safety standards, many major retailers also require samples to be submitted for their own testing prior to accepting shipments. While this adds time and cost to the production process, it's inevitable. It's estimated by manufacturers that in recent years with heightened requirements and additional testing by retailers, testing has added as much as 15% to the cost of a toy. While these added costs have generally been absorbed into the production and costing process at this point (2013), they have impacted every stage of product development from costing to timing to production.

This is further complicated by the fact that there are no constant safety standards across different countries. The European Union has different standards than South America or even the United States, and toys must comply in the countries they're being shipped to. The International Council of Toy Industries, which was formed in 1975, as a part of its mission to support the global toy business, eliminates barriers to trade and fosters social responsibility, and has addressed the need for global safety standards, but to date this has not been accomplished.

## Manufacturing

With very few exceptions, all products are manufactured overseas in Asia. Much manufacturing is concentrated in Guangzhou and Shenzhen in China, though there are manufacturing facilities in Vietnam, Cambodia, Sri Lanka, India and other areas. In the case of large toy companies, these companies either own factories or have partnerships with established factories to make the toys. Smaller companies usually source manufacturing by finding companies that specialize in different manufacturing processes.

Toys run the gamut of manufacturing processes from sewing for dolls or doll clothes to various plastics molding processes to wood, metal fabrication, electronic components and much more. In some cases, pieces are sourced from one manufacturer and put into a toy. For instance, rather than creating the molds and producing dice for a game, a game company may go to a factory that makes dice and either buy some already made or ask that company to make a customized set for the game. All of these elements figure into the costing process, with the overall objective to make the best toy possible for the least amount of money. Large toy companies may also buy futures, that is pay a set price for raw materials that have yet to be produced. This is particularly common with plastics that are petroleum based with costs that are variable. It's certainly one way to hedge bets on cost increases. This is also a tactic that's been used with computer chips.

Once the design has been finalized, the toy company's production and operations teams go through the process of putting together the components of the product, scheduling the manufacturing and assembly. Depending on the product, this can take anywhere from 3 to 6 months, or more. Unforeseen shortages of computer chips, an increasingly common problem for example, can slow production. Safety concerns or engineering problems can similarly slow the process. Ultimately, though the product is complete and ready to ship. Of course, this is a gross simplification of the entire process, and further study of manufacturing is recommended for anyone in the product end of this business.

# CHAPTER 4

# Buying and Selling

Even people who have been in the toy industry for their entire careers scratch their heads when it comes to the process of selling in to retailers. No matter the size of the company or the size of the order, no two deals are going to be identical. Nonetheless, there are some common elements that define this process consistently, and this chapter is intended to provide an introduction to that. It bears noting again that, as many industry insiders say, "you'll never know this till you live it," so what follows is in many respects an outline, but it should give a sense of what toy companies are up against as they try to get the finished product into retailers.

The so-called toy year, however, remains fairly constant in terms of its structure. Assuming that by the time you've got a product to the prototype stage, which can be as little as a few months or as long as a year depending on the product, there is still another year to go until the product hits the shelves.

This is where the retailers come in. Today, the mass-market toy landscape is dominated by Wal-Mart, Target, Toys "R" Us, and, increasingly, Amazon. Together, these four retailers account for approximately three-quarters of all the toys sold in the United States each year.

For most toys, the drop-dead date to be on shelf for the all-important holiday buying season is October 1. So let's go back in the process and work our way forward. Bear in mind that there will always be exceptions, but the following schedule is a good overall outline.

In June of the previous year, manufacturers met with retailers to show concepts and early prototypes. This is usually the first time manufacturers can begin gauge retailers' interest in a concept or a product. (If it's a line extension or something to do with an entertainment brand, it's possible that the product might have been presented earlier in a concept stage.)

From June through October, there is ongoing dialogue between the manufacturer and the retailer, but for the most part this is when concepts will be refined, prototypes built, and marketing programs beginning to be developed.

October is the time when retailers make initial commitments to products. This is when retailers are creating plan-o-grams, trying to determine what they're going to carry for the next year and how it will be merchandised. The early weeks of October are devoted to the Fall Preview show in Dallas and meetings with larger manufacturers at their facilities and showrooms. This is the time when retailers review what they saw in June, see how the products have developed and start slotting products and lines into their next year's plans. The last weeks of October are spent in Hong Kong further refining products and designs. Very often this process of refinement and negotiation continues through December.

Wal-Mart and Target, very often, wish to be able to finish their buying by December for the following holiday season, with Amazon and Toys "R" Us finishing up in the early part of the year. (Well, perhaps "buying" is not the right word. The retailers will commit to certain products, but they may not make confirmed orders till the early part of the following year, sometimes as late as April.) The challenge on both sides of this is that at this point, both manufacturers and retailers have no idea how the holiday season is going to end up, so in some cases that can mean planning to carry a product for a second year, or a line extension, before one has an idea of how the current year is going to end up.

So, as January arrives, it's not a done deal yet, for even as the major retailers are determining quantities and final costing, the round of international Toy Fairs begins. There are three major Toy Fairs that affect the U.S. Market. In Hong Kong, January is a time when buyers review product, and manufacturers work with the factories to refine pricing, sourcing materials, and beginning the manufacturing process—even though final quantities may not yet have been determined.

Late in January or early February, the industry decamps to Nuremburg—the largest of the international Toy Fairs. Again, the retailers and buyers meet, fine points of deals are drawn up, but the orders may not be forthcoming yet. Finally in February, the American International Toy Fair in New York is yet another chance to review product and refine deals.

## A Word About Toy Fairs

The American International Toy Fair began in 1903, and with the exception of 1 year during World War II, it has been run every year. As recently as the 1980s, the show ran for almost 2 weeks as retailers and toy companies sat down and worked through all the elements of a deal.

In recent years, with the shift to doing much of the work online and with dedicated executives visiting each of the major retailers individually, the function of Toy Fair has changed.

Today, for the larger, publicly traded manufacturers it is a chance to meet with the investment community and the media. For buyers, it's a chance to fill out the rest of their orders based on what they've bought from the major manufacturers.

For small toy companies, however, the New York Toy Fair is still very much a selling show. It's also the opportunity for smaller retailers to see the major toy companies. However, what these smaller retailers are able to buy are what the larger retailers have committed to. Major toy manufacturers need the volume commitment a major retailer can make to even begin to be able to create a mass-market toy profitably.

That said, Toy Fair is full of small toy companies, each trying to break into the industry. In fact, more than 1,600 exhibitors show at the New York Toy Fair every year, and the vast majority of these are smaller companies selling to the specialty marketplace.

It is these smaller companies that keep the American Toy Fair vital. For larger companies, the annual question is whether or not it makes sense to be there. For now, the answer continues to be yes, as it is the one U.S. showcases for what's new and innovative in the industry. Certainly, some companies do not show because they're privately held and do not sell to the smaller, specialty channels. But the demise of Toy Fair in New York has been foretold for the past decade, and it's still here. For all the advances in selling and communications, there still is not a more comprehensive way for buyers to get a sense of the scope of what is being offered.

Maddening as it may sound—and it is—when manufacturers work with the major retailers, there really is never any such thing as a finished deal. Toys will be ordered and made, and they'll be shipped to distribution centers and even put on shelves, but there are still other factors that can affect the final numbers.

For the most part, however, retailers need to make initial commitments by the end of March or early April at the latest. That's the only way to ensure that products can be manufactured and shipped in time for Q4 sales. Goods need to be in retailers' warehouses by mid-July to August. That's when the final merchandising of the department is set, and in some cases, toys can get into the stores so that retailers can get an early read on how a product might do.

The March/April timeframe is also when retailers and manufacturers begin planning promotions and advertising and figuring out which products they're going to be pushing for Q4.

There can also be cases where the entire process is moved earlier so that retailers can get an early read on a product in June to try to gauge how a product is going to do in the fourth quarter. Other products may be on shelf in August and early September to get an early read as well.

This puts special pressure on the manufacturers to advertise product and try to create a sensation in a time of year when people aren't necessarily buying toys. It can work, but the challenge is that a heavy ad schedule might cause a bump in sales for a 2- to 3-week test period, but it's impossible to keep that momentum going due to the amount of spending required to roll out that level of advertising nationally in the holiday season when advertising time is less available and more expensive.

But here's the catch. Once toys start to be on the shelf early and retailers get a read, two things happen. Retailers start chasing products that they think are going to be hot, and they start to cancel orders or shipments for products they think may not work.

In the chase scenario, an early sell-out with a marketing program that can be replicated in Q4 will mean that a major retailer will start trying to up their orders. At this point, however, the realities of production start to figure into the equation. In many cases, it's simply not possible to make and ship products in time for the holiday season, though sometimes inventory can be shipped by air instead of sea, which may cut weeks off the delivery but add exponentially to the cost. Generally once the orders are as close to final as can be, a manufacturer will allocate inventory to a customer and that may be all they will be able to get. Over the past several years, retailers have been wary about over-committing to quantities, which has shifted the risk to the manufacturers. As the manufacturers tell it, retailers only want to commit to a certain number of pieces, but if something takes off, they naturally want to be able to restock quickly. This puts the manufacturer in the position of trying to figure out whether to produce more products than have been ordered—and how many—at the risk of being left with excess inventory that will have to be liquidated in one way or another.

In the cancel scenario, a general rule of thumb is that toys have about 6 weeks to demonstrate their viability at retail. (As with everything we've discussed, this is a changeable figure based on the toy, relationship with the manufacturer and other factors.) However, at the point at which a retailer decides that a toy isn't going to perform up to its projections, while it may be too late to cancel orders on goods they've already taken, they can begin to cancel further shipments. Say, for example, that a toy doesn't do well in its first weeks, the retailer will do two things. First, it will discount the merchandise to try to clear the shelves, and second, it will cancel further shipments, such as those that might come in November. In many cases, that inventory is manufactured and landed in the United States. Again, the risk is shifted to the manufacturer who must figure out what to do with that merchandise.

To hear manufacturers talk about it, today's toy retailers are not merchants so much as risk managers, and to a certain degree that's true. No retailer wants to be left with a product that doesn't sell, and given that the toy industry is so unpredictable, the risk is very high. As we've repeatedly said, they're gambling on the whims of a 6-year-old. Typically buyers won't get punished for not buying something. If it's a hit, they can always sign on later. (This is particularly true of Wal-Mart, which in some cases can wait and see if something is going to become popular and then be pivotal in broadening the distribution greatly, as happened with Monster High.) On the other hand, taking a big position on a product that doesn't produce can saddle retailers with inventory that negatively affects profitability. This is also why initial negotiations can be so tough and grueling and why virtually any toy purchasing decision from a retailer today also includes a conversation about an exit strategy.

From the retailers' perspective, however, their primary objective is to satisfy their customers by offering the products they want. Essentially, a brick-and-mortar retailer is selling shelf space, and the question always has to be whether or not it's giving the best return possible. Since not all products in the department will have the same margin, can they deliver the right margin mix that will satisfy financial objectives and please investors, whether it's a public or private company?

This is why so many of the factors go into a purchase decision encompass much more than just the desire to put a piece of plastic on a shelf and hope that someone buys it. And that's why the industry works on such a tight time schedule. Buyers want to wait to commit until they have all the information possible so that they can make the most informed gamble when they finally make that commitment.

So, let's look at some of the factors that go into the purchasing decisions:

## Margins

In the years after World War II and even up until the 1970s, most often toys at retail were "keystoned." That is, retailers simply doubled the wholesale price and that was that. However, as toys changed and became more sophisticated and as advertising and promotion costs soared and the competition for the toy dollar became more heated and production costs rose, new formulas were required.

In today's market, margins can vary by item or line, and the goal for a retailer is to get an aggregate margin for an entire toy business of between 30% and 35%. How this is sliced up between and among the various products that a retailer carries is an ongoing challenge and why the spreadsheet is the best friend of both retailers and manufacturers.

Again, there are no hard and fast rules, but one can assume that lower priced items often deliver higher margins. However, even when a retailer is able to keystone an item, the volume required to come anywhere near the money generated by a higher end item at a 30% margin offsets the impact of the higher margin.

Categories that typically offer higher than average margins include arts and crafts, impulse toys, basics that don't have a license and basic toys within a larger brand. These tend not to be the "hot" items or the heavily promoted items, and, of course, there are always anomalies when something like Silly Bands take off, and consumers are suddenly paying $7 for 10 rubber bands, a product so commoditized outside of the toy world that Staples sells them by the pound or fraction of a pound.

At the end of the day, the deciding point in determining margin is the final price to the consumer. As we continue to see, there are price thresholds consumers simply won't pass, but these, too, are dynamic. In the late 1970s, a feature doll couldn't be sold for more than $14.99, until several came along that sold at $19.99, and that price was reset in consumers' minds.

So, let's look at a hypothetical case in round numbers. Let's say we've got a toy that's going to sell at $25. This could potentially be sold to the retailer for $12.50, and the retailer would, indeed, be able to get a keystoned mark-up on the product. However, let's consider that the product may have a hot, entertainment license on it, which can add 15% to the cost in royalty rates, so now that $12.50 to the retailer becomes about $14.50. Add another 15% for advertising and marketing (which can be conservative for a new introduction), and now we're at $16.50. That leaves you with close to your 30% margin. Then, let's assume that this particular toy is going to be price-promoted in the store advertising as a means of driving traffic or attracting customers, and the retailer wants to be able to discount the toy by about 15% in a key period, so now retail price is about $21.50. Suddenly, the margin on this toy has dropped to approximately 24%, below the number the retailer has to hit, and so that percentage and dollar volume has to be made up by other items in the store. This is easier to do when the toy in question is part of an entire line, say for an entertainment property, where there are other toys that will deliver higher margins as they won't have the advertising or promotional costs built in. It's assumed that the "key driver" may, in fact, deliver a significantly smaller margin overall, but that is compensated for by high volume sales of the key driver and sales of the other products in the line. The retailer is going to take it because his customers are going to be demanding it and expecting to find it in his toy department, so taking a hit on the margin is offset by the supposed increase in traffic and sales overall as customers look for that product. Of course, this only works if the sales all fall in line. When they do, everyone makes money and the gamble pays off, but they don't always work out that way.

In recent years, one of the major challenges to these equations has been the wide variation in pricing and price competition. Supporters of these tactics consider that this is just good old free market economics at work. Those who are negatively affected by it consider it "predatory pricing." Manufacturers can't set pricing; that's for the retailers to do, but there are consequences that affect profitability and the longer-term viability of a toy.

Here's what happens. A toy is considered hot and popular and may be getting a heavy advertising and PR push. Suddenly, consumers want it, and they head out to buy. As a means of attracting those consumers, one retailer cuts the price (an unplanned cost that hasn't been factored into the overall marketing and cost plan). Suddenly others follow suit, and a price war ensues. In recent years, this has been exacerbated by the ability of online merchants to cut costs throughout their system with a few clicks. While this may ultimately be good for the retailer, who is pursuing a market-basket strategy and intends to make up the lost margin on all of the other items a shopper buys, it can be devastating for a toy company because it devalues the toy overall, and while it won't affect toys that are already sold, it may have an impact on re-orders as retailers go back to demand reduced prices. This is also why so many toys only last one season. It's hard to go back to the well when the prices have been cut to the point that to maintain the reduced retail price would mean either a loss for the manufacturer, or a selling price that doesn't justify production.

Again, every toy is different, and every retailer is different, which brings us back to the aforementioned spreadsheets. It's only by careful and almost daily monitoring and quick actions that retailers and manufacturers can respond to market conditions either to take advantage of opportunities or address problems. The challenge, of course, as noted with the pricing example above, at times the goals of the two are at odds.

### *When Things Go Wrong—The Exit Strategy*

As noted earlier, most toy sales in the current marketplace come with an exit strategy. If a toy doesn't work or isn't selling up to expectations, it's imperative for the retailer to get out of it or minimize damage as quickly as possible. Once they get on the shelf, most retailers give a toy about 6 weeks to perform. However, there are cases where after a week when product didn't move, retailers want to get out. As we discussed earlier, this is all part of the risk-averse nature of the business and the need for space at retail to perform.

The first thing that happens when a toy doesn't do as expected is that the retailers mark down the toy and hope that a more price conscious consumer will purchase it. This is distinct from planned promotions where a toy will be available at a discounted price for a certain amount of time. Those special sales are usually calculated into the overall plan and pricing for the toy.

At the point at which a toy is marked down due to what is perceived to be poor performance, the retailer will ask the manufacturer for markdown money. Now, the last thing that a manufacturer wants to do is write a check to the retailer. The more common practice is that the retailer will provide a discount of anywhere from 2% to 5% if the invoice is still open.

The reason to do this, of course, is that it's essential for the manufacturer to maintain a good relationship with the retailer. Manufacturers need the retailers to buy from them the following year, so being as accommodating as possible is essential for relationship maintenance. Buyers have a great deal of power, and their decisions can affect not just the current year's sales but the relationship going forward.

There are other tactics that retailers employ, including sales promotions where customers get deep discounts on a second product if they buy the first one. They can move an under-performing product to a more prominent position and highlight the markdown. The goal is to get the inventory out of the store and off the balance sheet as quickly as possible.

There are many factors that can affect retail sales. From the retailer side, getting product on the shelves in time to coincide with the advertising breaking can affect them. From the manufacturer side concerns about early sales may lead them to cancel advertising to save money, but that will depress sales. If a product is based on an entertainment property, if that fails to catch on, the toys won't sell. Or, if product is on the way to a retailer and suddenly the release date for a movie changes, that has an impact all the way up the chain. And the very fashion-oriented, whim-driven nature of the market makes it unpredictable. One would like to say that the goal posts keep moving. The fact of the matter in the toy industry, however, is that nobody really knew where the goal posts were in the first place.

This is why veterans of this industry say you can't really understand how the sales process works till you've lived it. To a certain extent that may be true. However, the process is one of constantly juggling numbers and reassessing on an almost daily basis to maximize every opportunity and minimize every setback.

### *When the Market is Short*

In the current marketplace, costing, projections and forecasts need to be made based on 1 year's sales. Remember, since 40% of the market will be new every year, the chance to continue a product for a second year has become increasingly challenging.

Coming up with the correct inventory levels is always more an art than a science, but generally manufacturers manufacture fairly close to their sales numbers to avoid carrying over inventory.

In situations where something becomes a hit, or even a fad, there is going to be a shortage of product in the marketplace. In recent years, this has been helpful to try to get a second or even third year out of a product. We discussed Mattel's Monster High earlier and that not all retailers got on board. When it became a hit, it quickly sold out while demand was still high. While no one likes to leave money on the table, Mattel's shorting of the market created ongoing demand that has allowed the line to go into a third year with a great deal of momentum behind it.

Similarly, LeapFrog's LeapPad tablet was short in its first year, creating a demand that lasted into a second year and has remained strong, even as the second generation was introduced.

Neither of these was necessarily planned. The companies manufactured to the orders that they had and demand simply outstripped supply. However, both companies benefitted from the attention they got in the news media and from word of mouth as one of the "hard to find" toys of their launch years. By selling out and leaving consumers wanting more, both companies had a chance to manage their products and seed new products into the market at the pace of demand, creating an ongoing revenue stream—at least for at time. (At this writing both are still going strong, but the inevitable cycle of the toy market will ultimately render them obsolete.)

At this point, however, a product needs to be managed carefully or else it's more than possible to kill the proverbial golden goose. Take, for example, Zhu Zhu pets. They became an incredible hit and a fad. Demand was through the roof and supply was low. However, going into a second year, Cepia flooded the market with product and essentially killed it. Both the retailers and the manufacturers misread the demand and rather than keeping supply low over time created a situation where the market was quickly saturated—and left a lot of inventory on the shelves. (We'll discuss fads futher on.)

### *Expanding Retail Channels*

Much has been written and said about the consolidation of the toy industry over the past decades. Indeed, with Wal-Mart, Target, Toys "R" Us and Amazon dominating the business, the stakes at each retailer are significantly higher than they were when there were more retail outlets. Manufacturers weren't as dependent on three or four major retailers.

In today's market, there are more channels carrying toys. Drug stores have begun carrying mainstream toys. Supermarkets carry toys and stores like Kohl's are also stocking toys. The discount clubs—Sam's Club, BJ's, etc.—stock toys, but many of those are exclusive products.

### *Exclusives*

One of the most competitive areas of the toy industry in recent years has been the fight for exclusives. Retailers, especially the big box chains, want toys that are exclusive to them. This gives them a competitive advantage to be sure and, at the same time, frees them from the competitive pricing practices described earlier.

Exclusives are hotly negotiated in the buying process. And they come in different forms that, you guessed it, can vary by retailer.

Historically exclusives were relatively simple. There might be a different decoration for one store versus another, or a specific grouping of products in a co-pack that is different from store to store. In the current marketplace, the exclusive can be a key to a retailer's overall merchandising strategy.

It's rare that a key driver for a company will be offered as an exclusive. One retailer may get it exclusively for a 6-week window, where the product is launched. More common is an exclusive item in an established line.

For the retailers, though, exclusives do not necessarily come cheap. Manufacturers can charge more, but then so can the retailers. The retailer is also expected to put more promotion behind the product. This can mean featured placement in the store, inclusion in store advertising, featured placement in newspaper sections, inclusion on the store's holiday hot lists and more.

Exclusives can be great for smaller companies who are trying to get a foothold in the business as well. Production quantities are lower and placement is assured, making it possible to plan a little more effectively. They also provide a kind of test market where if a product succeeds it will be easier to open the door to broader distribution.

## *Fads*

Fads can never be planned for. They happen every so often, but from Shirley Temple dolls to Twister to Wizzzers to Cabbage Patch dolls to Beanie Babies to Tickle Me Elmo to Furby and so on, these are the toys that transcend any kind of rational marketing and become part of the culture. We're not concerned here with the sociology of a fad here, but rather the impact of a fad on the toy business overall.

No two fads have ever begun the same way, but in the fads since the 1980s, they have all behaved fairly similarly in the market. Some event triggers awareness and popularity outside of a traditional toy market. Bryant Gumble playing with Tickle Me Elmo on the Today Show and Rosie O'Donnell doing the same on hers are credited with jumpstarting the craze for that toy in 1996. Suddenly there's a run on the toy at retail, news media report on it, and it's off and running.

For both manufacturers and retailers, the goal is to get as much product into the pipeline while the demand is white-hot. Scarcity, of course, triggers more news stories, which triggers more demand, which triggers the video of people fighting in the aisles of toy stores and so on.

These fads tend to happen in the fourth quarter as people are trying to get products for the holiday, and especially for a complex product, gearing up production and shipping can be a challenge. When all of those factors are considered, it's feasible that a retailer and a manufacturer may make very little money on a fad item—or actually lose money. Still, the fad drives store traffic and traditionally has boosted other, unrelated toy sales.

Fads inevitably die down as the holiday season passes and public attention switches to other issues. What happens next, though, can be critical. Even as the fad—and the media attention—dies down, there is an opportunity for extended sales. Tickle Me Elmo and Furby both sold more units in their second years than in their first, fad-driven years. The challenge for a manufacturer is to maintain strict control over inventory levels so that availability can keep pace with demand. As noted above, when Zhu Zhu Pets flooded the market in the second year, the excess inventory met the demand, which didn't increase. Tickle Me Elmo, and subsequent versions of Elmo, became a staple of the preschool plush business. Furby went on to sell more than 40 million units and sold 14 million toys in its second year with distribution expanded around the globe after only selling about 1.8 million in its first.

Still, as great as that was for Hasbro, the company's ability to respond to the fad was critical—and to leverage it strategically in a second year. Similarly, Fisher-Price managed the Elmo property over many years, introducing Elmo's that did a variety of different things—Hokey Pokey, Chicken Dance, etc.—and after a first year of sales, sold them exclusively through Toys "R" Us. The multiple years are, of course, where the extended profitability is once design and tooling costs have been largely amortized and margins can be higher.

Fads can be powerful, but as noted, they can't be planned for. The factors that contribute to a fad are so outside what any manufacturer or retailer can ever control that thinking of them as anything other than a phenomenon is pointless. And, anyone who promises that they can create a fad (and there are marketers who do) is blowing smoke.

### The Specialty Market

The focus of this introduction has largely been on the mass market that sells about 80–85% of the toys in the United States. The so-called specialty sector is actually loosely defined and generally covers smaller, independent merchants who carry product that is not highly promoted, educational in nature and so forth. With retail sales of approximately $3 billion annually, the industry is represented by the American Specialty Toy Retailing Association (ASTRA), and they promote the toys they represent as having fewer electronics and more play value, are of higher quality and are less likely to have licensed characters.

These toys are often bought for younger children or when parents are controlling the spending and often as a counterpoint to more highly promoted mainstream toys.

The market is, and is likely to remain, very small as a function of the entire toy industry in the United States, but depending on the toys, this channel can be a relatively low risk test market for a toy that might have potential to go mainstream. Probably the most successful category for potential crossover is games where a large manufacturer can provide a game with distribution that a smaller operation could not.

That said, all of the tests of viability apply as for mass-market toys. And, while specialty toys are generally more expensive for the consumer, the common perception is that the value is higher—at least among those who buy. Independent retailers also expect to have higher margins on the toys they sell, given the limited retail space and the need for profitability per square foot.

Many small companies have their own sales personnel, but many also work through distributors. Given the shrinking of the overall retail marketplace for toys in recent years, the number of distributors has decreased, but going through regional distributors is the only way they can reach potential retailers. For these manufacturers, too, Toy Fairs still play a very important role in finding new channels of distribution.

Independent retailers also, as you might expect, place smaller orders. It's common for orders of as little as a few dozen, so the need to make many of those small sales is self-evident.

Larger manufacturers generally do not service these retailers. Instead, they work almost exclusively through distributors for them. The challenge, of course, is that there is no way that an independent retailer can compete with a mass merchant on price so the overlap of product is rare.

The exception is Toys "R" Us. Strictly speaking, Toys "R" Us *is* a specialty retailer since they specialize in toys. Yet, in its scale and pricing structure they act like a big box retailer. Through their Imaginarium brand and their FAO Schwarz enterprise, as well as in their basics business, they can offer a broader variety of toys that will attract that so-called specialty customer. In addition, Toys "R" Us carries approximately 7,000 different toys, while Wal-Mart or Target may only carry about 1,200. The opportunities for a smaller toy company are, obviously, better at Toys "R" Us.

Online is quickly transforming the specialty sector, however. Amazon has recently moved into this arena as well, as they can easily broaden their offerings without adding to space at retail. Amazon, and to a certain extent eBay, also provide platforms for independent retailers to get into the online business, though this is highly competitive and more vulnerable to price competition than a single beloved store in a specific market. As more and more toy buyers are researching and purchasing toys online, the opportunity for broader distribution is greater for the specialty manufacturers while creating a more challenging competitive environment for the specialty retailer.

## An Exception to the Rule—Withholding: A New Strategy in Launching Product

By this point, you should know that there are exceptions to every "rule" in the toy industry. One that is becoming increasingly common for toy companies of all sizes is withholding information from retailers early on in the process and only showing them product when it's nearly fully developed. Yes, there may still be time to make changes, but they are not brought into the fold as early as they are on some other products.

This is a business that has, certainly since the 1970s, been characterized by secrecy, and in the current marketplace to show something to one retailer is virtually the same as making a public announcement. Thus, companies have begun holding back items from this overall process and only revealing them to retailers at a point where the development is so far along that it's virtually impossible for another company to come in and knock it off. Yes, knock-offs are a problem in the toy industry and the not-unfounded concern is that if a toy company reveals something to Retailer A, for instance, that retailer may approach another company and ask for something similar at a lower cost. The challenge is always that one cannot trademark an idea, merely the expression of an idea. So, as a defensive strategy, manufacturers are bringing retailers into the process later. Now, this is not true for all items, but only for key drivers or things a company may think could be a breakout hit. What this gains is the ability to be a first mover in the marketplace. It took about a year for other supernatural dolls to follow Monster High. What it loses is the retailers' participation in the development process. However, that, too, can be offset by a track record of success. If Hasbro is introducing an innovative NERF item, based on their long-running success with that brand, or Mattel is unveiling a new fashion doll, retailers may be more likely to be willing to wait and place their orders when they find out what the product is.

To an industry outsider, this can create a kind of cloak-and-dagger impression, complete with secret back rooms in showrooms, or items not even shown at Toy Fairs, but given the competitive nature of the market and the scramble for every dollar—to say nothing of being able to capitalize on a competitive company's research and development—it's somewhat necessary. And it does add a level of intrigue to the business; there's no denying that.

# CHAPTER 5

# Creating Desire: Licensing, Advertising & Marketing

Getting the toys on the shelf is only half the battle. Getting them off the shelves and into the hands of consumers is another. Remember, as we mentioned earlier, at the end of the day no one really *needs* a toy. So, the ultimate challenge of any objective of any marketing program is to create the perception of a need where none exists. What follows is an introduction to the various processes and strategies companies use to try to get their products off the shelves and into the hands of consumers.

Marketing is expensive, and the costs need to be factored in up front. Once again, the toy industry is hard to quantify in this way. In typical consumer package goods businesses, companies might have an advertising-to-sales ratio of 10–15%. In other words that percentage of projected first year sales would be dedicated to marketing, often TV advertising.

With toys, however, that ratio may need to be significantly higher in the first—and sometimes only—year. It's crowded market, and in today's market that requires a mix of strategies and tactics to get attention. From timing the launch to creating exclusives, to producing television ads, to licensing to online, all of these factor into the contemporary toy market. As the TV market becomes more fragmented, finding where the eyes are, as the saying goes, is increasingly challenging. That's why marketing strategies need to be set early on in the production cycle—and followed through. The closeout bins of toy stores across the land are chock full of toys that started strong but suffered when marketing was cut back. The risk is always that the money invested in development, sales, and merchandising may be lost because a marketer got cold feet.

But in today's toy market, engaging in some kind of marketing—and often highly aggressive marketing—is not an option. This is a promotion-responsive industry, and too often toymakers ignore or cut back marketing expenditures prematurely. Time and again, one sees that cutting back marketing can be done for many reasons. Perhaps a company wants to make numbers for a particular quarter. Saving a couple of million dollars in advertising expense can be very helpful. Perhaps a company is concerned that a toy hasn't done well in its first few weeks of release, and rather than backing their bet, they pull back. There are virtually no cases one can cite where pulling back from marketing has been beneficial to a product where there is not momentum for a product in the marketplace.

Consider a now-defunct toy company, DSI. DSI invested heavily in a licensed product targeted to tweens (kids ages 8–11). They signed an expensive licensing deal with a flash-in-the-pan celebrity and went into production on the toy. As often happens in the toy industry, at least to this observer, exuberance for the toy and the celebrity involvement trumped more strategic planning and the validation process was virtually skipped. They relied on the power of a celebrity to pull the toy through retail rather than doing more in-depth research. (Celebrity dolls have done well, but they are a comparatively quick in and out business, and a volatile one at that. More than one celebrity doll has been cut from the line when the real-life celebrity got into hot water for various reasons.) The process became more and more expensive, and the company needed to cut costs. The easiest place to cut costs was in marketing because those funds hadn't yet been spent. But that is also probably the most foolish because if no one knows about the toy, no one can develop a preference for the toy, and the result is no sales. All the developmental money is down the drain. After this, the company soon went out of business. Now, there were other factors, but certainly a failure to follow through when in some respects the company has bet the farm on a product and then doesn't support it was a major contributor.

When does it work to cut marketing? Certainly with hit toys, there's no need to spend money where it's not needed. Whether it's Tickle Me Elmo, Furby, or any other toy that has significant momentum behind it, a savvy company redirects marketing dollars into products and categories that need the push. Even with a product that is not a fad, when a promoted product is going to sell through in a season, there comes a point where marketing has done its job, and companies can pull back.

Like the other aspects of the toy industry, this is more an art than a science, and it requires constant monitoring to make the most effective use of resources. Of course, when a company has other objectives than moving product, that's going to change.

Any discussion of marketing in the toy industry needs to start with looking at the "toy dollar," that is the amount of money that is spent on non-essential, leisure products targeted to children. The discussion also requires a look at the toy buyers and purchase occasions.

## The "Toy Dollar"

We talk about the "toy dollar" as a kind of collective phrase designed to identify money consumers spend on non-essential, leisure items. In the 1950s and 1960s, that was mostly on toys, hence the name, but today the term refers to discretionary spending on products designed for kids to use in their leisure time.

In the years after the end of World War II, the toy business virtually stood on its own as separate and distinct. That began to change with the greater penetration of transistor radios as entertainment for kids in the early 1960s and certainly with the introduction of video games. For the most part, however, toys were toys and the crossover between kids' products and adults' products was relatively minimal.

That all changed with the growth of the home computer in the late 1970s, the introduction in 2001 of the iPod and the steady expansion of the cell phone market. Over the last decade that's only increased as technology has become more and more part of everyday life. The difference, of course, is that kids are completely adept at and at-home with adult technology, eliminating what was once a barrier between kids' products and adult products. The two are often now interchangeable.

Although for several years it was fashionable for companies and marketing consultants to talk about Kids Getting Older Younger (KGOY) to explain why kids were moving away from traditional toys, the toy industry hasn't suffered from the expansion of technology, as noted by constant sales performance year over year. This concept is largely meaningless, and was employed as a way of explaining how someone missed the market.

Rather, a facility with technology may mean that adults and children have products in common, but they use them in distinctly different ways, making the overall toy box larger, to speak somewhat poetically. Kids do move beyond traditional toys by about age 8, but at the same time, innovations in radio control, new games, building sets, and many more categories have continued to thrive largely because they deliver an experience that can't be replicated by a technology. There may, for example, be coloring apps that can be used on a tablet, but that doesn't replace a child's desire to color with crayons. Moreover, when one considers the success of toy tablets like LeapFrog's LeapPad or VTECH's Innotab, one sees that one of the fundamental characteristics of toys remains unchanged: toys replicate the adult world in a way that is appropriate for children. Kids still want to feel "big." A facility with technology does not necessarily mean an increased cognitive ability. Indeed, Kids' cognitive and physical development have not accelerated in any measurable way in the past 50 years. The mistake that many adults make is to look at kids playing with the same things they use and infer that the child is more sophisticated than is truly the case. (Remember how amazed your grandparents were that you knew how to fix the clock on the VCR? Children encounter and adapt to the world they're in, and to some adults that can look like brilliance when it's simply a not-very-special part of these children's world.)

Still, a broader range of products competing for discretionary dollars means that competition is more intense than it was a decade ago, and that competition is not always logical. Marketers have to realize that the competition is neither direct nor necessarily logical as it might be between different brands of toothpaste, for instance. The toy dollar can go many places today that defies typical market research. Looking at the competitive field, it's never apples-to-apples. It's apples-to-peaches-to-outboard motors.

One of the impacts of this exploding competitive field is the way technology has also changed price sensitivity among consumers, which can be both good and bad for toymakers. On the one hand, higher prices for technology make toys seem more reasonable overall. Over time—dating from the 1990s forward—consumer perception of what is reasonable to spend has increased. This has been particularly true with electronic accessories where $20 is considered an impulse buy, as opposed to a planned purchase. While this is not true across the board, the comparative price of toys versus other more expensive toys that kids want has made parents more open to spending more frequently at the lower end.

On the other hand, toy consumers have become more sensitive at the higher end of toy purchases. Toy buyers begin to see an expensive toy as competitive with other, more expensive products, such electronics, even when they are not directly competitive, serve a different function for the child and may cost a great deal more. For example, when confronted with a $70 animated plush toy, consumers think, "Well, that's about half the price of an iPod Nano," and they begin to consider the relative value of two unrelated products, both of which their child wants. The inevitable price/value calculation that consumers do is vastly different than what an adult consumer does because he or she would not likely consider the purchase of a pair of shoes and a television competitive.

All of this makes the "toy dollar" hard to quantify in any consistent, or even logical, way, and, as we'll see, makes the challenge of the marketers more challenging than in other types of businesses.

## The Toy Consumer

Typically, there are two events in a child's year when he or she gets toys: birthday and a fourth quarter holiday.

And, of course, like everything else in the study, there is no consistent profile of the toy consumer. Anyone who buys toys fits the bill. So, really, the toy-buying public is as diverse as the population at large.

However, there are a few things to bear in mind about the intended recipients of toys.

For children under two, toys are selected by parents or adults. After two, children begin requesting toys, and with some exceptions, most toys during the next toy years are in response to direct requests. These requests are made in response to advertising, promotion, word-of-mouth and other forms of communications targeted to kids. The goal for marketers is to create the desire in the child. That desire becomes a perceived need. That perceived need becomes a request, and that request is either granted or denied by the adult who holds the purse strings.

The toy consumer is anyone who buys toys and anyone who plays with them, a fairly broad description to say the least. Not very helpful, right? As a result toymakers need to define the market for their toys as specifically as possible, always with the understanding of child development and cognitive abilities at different ages. As discussed earlier, these market segments are much narrower and finer than in the adult market. What a child can do at 18 months and at 3 years are vastly different; the kids aren't even really the same person at those ages. So, targeting the toy to the age and then determining the purchaser and the purchase occasion can let one refine the target and begin the process of driving purchases.

In the current economy, the toy consumer is also very price conscious and price savvy. The revolution in Smartphones is pushing this even further. It's now possible, for instance, for a consumer to scan a barcode in a store and look up pricing at different retailers, or purchase immediately online. At the very least this is causing conflict at retailers who are advertising price-matching programs, but it is also shifting the balance of power to the consumer who can choose to buy or not in an instant. Armed with information and a price comparison tool, today's toy buyer is a force to be reckoned with, rather than a customer to be dictated to.

## The Marketing Process

There is very little that is straightforward about the process of marketing toys. That should come as no surprise to anyone. The diversity of the markets, the changing nature of the media marketplace, and the rise of social media and technology have transformed the entire process.

Historically, TV advertising was the only way to go. In the 1960s when the bulk of the Baby Boom generation was consuming toys, kids were glued to one of three channels on a Saturday morning. A toymaker would put a toy on TV enough that kids would request the toy, and that would be that. The rise of cable TV and currently the move toward home video and subsequently recorded and streaming programming means that no one knows for sure "where the eyes are." We'll discuss targeting advertising in a little bit.

The fragmentation of the media market, particularly as it relates to kids' programming has necessitated use of other tactics—promotion, online, social media, etc. Today's promotional landscape is unlike anything we've seen in the past, and the traditional metrics and measurements don't necessarily apply.

It is, to use a cliché, a kind of Wild West atmosphere in the toy market right now. What works, if it works, is going to be different for every product and every program. But let's take a look at some of the general practices that are part of the mix.

## Licensing

Licensing as a marketing process dates back to the end of the 19th Century in toys. The first known character to appear on a toy was The Yellow Kid, a cartoon that ran from 1895 to 1898 in New York papers. The character was so popular that consumers wanted to bring it into their lives more than just in a comic strip.

That's been the essence of successful character and brand licensing for the past 105 years, or so. From Mickey Mouse to Shirley Temple to The Flintstones to The Six Million Dollar Man to Star Wars to Care Bears to South Park to Hello Kitty and so on and so on, characters that have captured popular imagination have been highly effective at moving product at retail. You'll also notice in the above list the diversity of characters and potential audiences. Successful character licensing is a powerful inducement to fans of the characters to purchase toys and all kinds of ancillary products from pins to apparel and much more. For our purposes, however, we're going to talk exclusively about toys.

The prominence of licensing in the contemporary toy industry dates from 1977 and the introduction of *Star Wars*. The runaway success of the product—and the success of selling empty boxes to consumers for holiday 1977 as a promise for what was to come—changed the business forever. Before *Star Wars*, licensed product based on entertainment properties was almost an afterthought, or at the very least was not part of the initial planning for a movie or television show.

In today's market, virtually every movie and TV show targeted to children has some kind of toy licensing program associated with it. Often, programs and content are designed specifically to create a toy or play experience. It may have a broader licensing program as discussed above, but for our purposes we will be speaking specifically about toy programs. These programs have greater or lesser success, but they all have certain things in common.

There are really two types of toy licensing agreements currently used: Master Toy and Category.

In a Master Toy agreement, a company secures the rights to all toys even if they don't produce toys in all categories targeted for inclusion. The Category license is for a specifically defined category, such as action figures or dolls. With the exception of the sub-licensing, initial deals with a property owner or licensor work pretty much the same.

The licensee pays an up-front guarantee designed to secure the license for a specific period of time and an agreed-upon royalty rate. The royalty rates are a percentage of net toy sales featuring the property.

A typical licensing agreement will include the following points:

- ☐ Brands and Trademarks (which trademarks are included)
- ☐ Release dates or air dates of entertainment, when relevant
- ☐ Product Categories for branding or brand extensions
- ☐ Term or length of the brand licensing agreement
- ☐ Contract Years (if the term is broken up by year)
- ☐ Sales Quota
- ☐ Upfront Payment/Minimum Guarantee
- ☐ Royalty Rate for the branded product
- ☐ Audit provision
- ☐ Distribution Channels for the brand
- ☐ Territory for the branded products
- ☐ Marketing Commitment for the licensing partnership
- ☐ Marketing and On-Shelf Dates for the licensed products
- ☐ Sell-Off Period

While many of these are fairly obvious and standard to any kind of licensing, there are some variables that are unique to toy licensing. Let's take a look at some of those and how they affect the toy business. This can be a very competitive field for many toy companies, so delineating these points can make a tremendous difference in the way product sells.

## Release Dates

Given the lead-time to produce toys and get them into the marketplace, the release dates are critical. Typically, toymakers plan to have toys related to movies on shelf approximately 6 weeks before the movie premieres. For certain movies such as the Batman series, Avengers, Transformers, and other franchises that have a broader appeal than just the usual juvenile toy consumer, these on-shelf dates play a critical role in promoting the movie and helping to build excitement about it in the culture.

Thus, delineating the date in the contract provides a commitment from both parties about the promotion of the property. A movie that is delayed, for example, can have a negative impact on a toymaker when it has planned sales, shipped product and so forth. Product that is either pulled from the shelf or languishes there gives the toymaker the opportunity to renegotiate future payments to compensate for its loss.

## Product Categories

This is one of the most often negotiated points in a licensing deal. The licensor wants to collect as many upfront guarantees as possible. This can lead to what is often referred to as "slice-ensing," slicing up a license so thinly that companies are in virtual competition with one another. A licensor, for example, can give a license to one company for 12-inch plush and another for 14-inch plush. A third company can get a license for feature plush and so on. The licensees are in competition with one another, if not in the mind of the licensor, at least in the reality of what a retailer can stock and end consumer perception. This is common primarily when there is competition for hot licenses.

## Distribution Channels

These can similarly be determined on an almost granular basis. The general distinctions, however, are mass market, specialty, gift, drug, and wholesale club. Taking our plush example above, a licensee could get the license for 12-inch plush in drug and be in competition with someone who has the license for 12-inch plush in gift channels. Clearly, the desire for the licensee is to get the broadest possible permission for channels. Still, there are certain manufacturers who specialize in specific channels, such as wholesale club or amusement, which are the large characters often seen as prizes on midways. Again, a licensor is only going to be highly restrictive when dealing with a hot property. In the case of a property that a licensor is trying to launch in the marketplace, the property owner may be eager to grant the broadest possible rights in order to entice the toymaker and, hopefully, the retailers to take a chance on an unproven property.

## Upfront Payment/Minimum Guarantee

This has been a dynamic area in the crafting of licensing agreements in recent years. Previously, an upfront guarantee based as a certain percentage of projected first year sales was *de rigeur*. Now, well, it depends.

A hot property or a potential blockbuster movie or the next movie in a franchise has a certain amount of momentum behind it, and while there are never any guarantees, it's a little easier to forecast, always knowing that traditionally subsequent movies in a series can expect lower retail sales.

As noted above with "slice-ensing," movie producers hope to get as much money as they can early on in the process to help fund production and marketing. When there is competition for a license, the licensor can demand large upfront payments. Though this practice has not been as widespread in recent years, largely due to the decline in the number of toy companies and retail channels, a licensor will always find a way to carve out part of a category for a potential licensee with a large amount of money to spend.

However, in recent years, this has changed, particularly when the goal is to launch a new property. In order to get product into the marketplace, licensors have increasingly been willing to reduce or forego upfront payments in order to get payment on the back end. This is truly a case of what the market will bear, since no two properties are directly competitive, so it's virtually impossible to set a standard.

In a situation where the licensee may waive the large upfront payment, they will require a minimum guarantee, which is the total amount of royalties that the licensee will pay during the terms of the contract. This helps the licensee particularly in the case of an unproven property. In a perfect world, that money saved by the licensee would go into product development, and it does allow the licensor and licensee to share a bit more of the risk.

## Royalty Rates

Today, royalty rates fluctuate depending on the property, the product category, the distribution channels and the upfront money.

Typically for an entertainment property those rates are between 12 and 15%, though they can go higher. Indeed, rates were in the low 20% range for properties like *Star Wars* when it demonstrated it's long-term selling ability and a willingness among consumers to pay a premium for these products.

Ironically, though, it was *Star Wars* that began the downward move of royalty rates when *Star Wars The Phantom Menace* toys didn't meet expectations.

In the current market, increased costs and pressure from retailers to keep prices low have kept royalty rates lower than their historic highs. Adding a huge charge, as a proportion of sales, at the front end makes it more challenging to sell product at an acceptable price for consumers. Like so much in the toy industry, each case requires a balance demand, product, price, and timing. All of these factors go into a licensing agreement, and they are all negotiable depending on the property.

In addition to character licensing, brands also figure in the toy industry, whether industrial brands like John Deere and Caterpillar, food brands like Coca-Cola or Slurpee, entertainment brands like NASCAR or others. These typically have lower royalty rates, which can hover around 7%. Again, this is negotiable based on the potential effectiveness of the brand in moving the needle in toy sales.

## Audit Provision

This is an often-overlooked component of a licensing contract. But all parties to a licensing contract should ensure their right to audit one another. Millions of dollars have been recovered on either side of an agreement in the audit process. Whether it's a licensee under-reporting sales or a licensor not fulfilling the promotional obligations of its contract, this can be a very high stakes process and ensuring the agreements are honored on both sides is critical.

## Sell-Off Period

As contracts end, as movies fade, and so forth, both parties to the agreement need to determine how to get rid of excess inventory. Terms vary, of course, but typically, a licensee has about 90 days to get rid of any unsold merchandise produced under the agreement.

Chances are that these goods will be sold at a reduced price, so there may be a stipulation for a reduced royalty during this time, often based on average rates under the contract or the latter portion of it. At the same time, the licensor wants to protect from a flood of goods at bargain basement prices, so a minimum price (a percentage of the original) may be stated. The licensor also doesn't want to be surprised by this, so the contract will usually state how the licensee provides information on inventory and timing for sell off. If the licensee has violated the contract, the licensor can also deny the sell-off period.

The licensee must often stop all production of licensed goods and offer the licensor the opportunity to purchase any remaining stock. Moreover, at the end of the sell-off period, any remaining merchandise must be destroyed. The sell-off period is when the audit clause becomes even more important. Relations between licensor and licensee may have seriously deteriorated during this period, particularly if a property has not done well.

Clearly, anyone seeking to enter a licensing agreement or grant one must think through all of the elements of the agreement, and there are attorneys who specialize in these agreements.

## Developing Products

In the best-case scenarios for licensed goods, the products are developed collaboratively between the licensee and licensor. Products that are most likely to be successful are those that make sense for the brand, naturally, which is defined for toys as creating situations where kids can reproduce elements of the property in their play. Whether it's taking on super powers, creating narrative-based scenarios or other types of activities, creating a good toy is essential. For years, many marketers simply applied a character sticker to an existing product, changed the decoration of a game or created a standard grouping of action figures or plush characters for the property. In the last 20 years or so, as the market has become more crowded, this practice has come to be known as "label slapping." While it certainly kept development costs down, it also hasn't worked in recent years. Trading on popularity isn't enough. Rather, toymakers need to create unique experiences that are directly relevant not just to the property but to the play pattern of the children who are the target audience. In today's market, a good licensed toy must first be a good toy, and licensors are becoming more and more demanding about the levels of play, technology and so forth, in the toys as there is greater competition among properties and for the share of a child's toybox.

Throughout the development process, licensors have the right to approve every aspect of the toy from design to molds to packages to commercials and so forth. Most properties have what is called a "bible" or style guide that outlines the characters, how they're seen from every angle, their characteristics, size relative to other characters in the property and much more. This is provided to the licensees and they are expected to follow it. Brands, too, have style guides that govern color usage, logo presentation, and much more. For the licensor, few things are as important as a consistent presentation of the property through all categories of merchandise.

## Selecting a Property

There are many considerations that go into selecting a property. While the licensing process is the same, the performance and behavior of different properties vary widely by the type of property, product category and the target audience.

Regardless of what type of property, anyone thinking of getting into this business has to create a strategic plan, always acknowledging that this is a highly competitive field, and one of the primary objectives at all levels of product and distribution is to minimize risk. Different categories bring with them different levels of risk, but a savvy licensee doesn't go into the market without doing an overall, cold-eyed market analysis to determine the audience, the competitive environment and the channels of distribution. The competitive analysis is especially important when a manufacturer is targeting mass-market distribution. It's important to identify where a property fits in the current, and ever-changing field, in order to determine viability and profitability.

Is it, for example, a long-term or a short-term play? Will a consumer walk across the store to see and perhaps purchase the product? Is it in the channels where the target customer is shopping? Will your category be compelling for fans of the property? Where are you in the life cycle of a property?

These last two questions are very important for toymakers. Is it a way that children want to encounter the property. Take, for example, the original products based on the Harry Potter movies. Action figures did all right, though games and roleplay items did much better. Given the popularity of the books and the anticipation for the movies, it was assumed that toys would do well across the board, but what the market ultimately demonstrated was that children who loved Harry Potter wanted to feel as though they had entered the world themselves, rather than playing with figures. Understanding the play pattern derived from a property is a key part of the upfront research. Of course, the studios will be eager to have products produced in every category, and given the diversity of the market there may be opportunities in each. The challenge for the licensee is to determine the potential of the different categories without respect to the desires of a studio. (There are situations where in order to get one category a licensee is required to take another, which is a way to get the widest presence of a property at retail, but quantities need to be estimated according to potential.) Remember, the most essential element of a property in the toy industry at least is that the narrative and the characters need to be so compelling to a child that he or she wants to include them in his or her play. At the same time, when one new property comes into a child's life, another usually goes.

Properties, like every fashion brand, have a life cycle. Understanding that cycle as it relates to a specific property and knowing where the property is in that cycle is essential to forecasting. There are evergreen properties, such as Hello Kitty, various Disney characters and properties that have become established such as Dora The Explorer and Pokémon. These have a demonstrated track record, which makes them a bit more predictable in terms of sales—as long as the product is right.

## The Wonder Forge—How Licensing Solved Marketing Problems

The Wonder Forge is a Seattle-based games company founded in 2007. Getting placement in the games business, especially in preschool games can be very challenging. Jacobe Chrisman, who runs the company and who had previously headed up product development at Cranium, knew that creating good games was only part of the equation the company needed. He realized that a licensing strategy was essential to break through—and get retailer placement.

However, the licensing strategy needed to be one that was sustainable, to the extent anything in the toy industry is, and Chrisman and his team secured licenses for Dr. Seuss, Curious George, Angelina Ballerina, Richard Scarry and more. The licenses were affordable, had definable target audiences and filled a void at retail.

As The Wonder Forge began to become known for delivering high-quality games and, most importantly, profits for retailers, the company expanded. Suddenly they found themselves in a very different position. With an infusion of capital in 2012, and a slew of awards, the company has been able to acquire even more high-profile licenses like Teenage Mutant Ninja Turtles, Disney Princesses and Minnie Mouse and establishing it as a go-to manufacturer for licensors.

Most importantly, licensing as a function of marketing has been critical to the Wonder Forge's success. Preschool games have price thresholds that make it virtually impossible to afford the level of TV advertising and promotion required to launch a game. In this case, the power of the properties in the mind of the consumers who are looking for varied ways for their children to engage with properties they love and the halo effect of the promotion and broader-based awareness of the properties in the marketplace overall becomes a critical factor in selling the games.

The success of the licensed games has allowed the company to expand into other types of games and products, though the privately held company is tightly managed and has concentrated primarily on classic and evergreen properties in its products.

Because different types of properties behave differently, let's take a quick look at some of the different types of properties out there.

## Movie Properties

For the most part, any blockbuster movie is going to have one of the larger toy companies as the Master Toy licensee, as described earlier. These are the companies—Mattel, Hasbro, Jakks Pacific, Spin Master, etc.—who are going to be able to put the product development and marketing resources behind the toys. They are also going to be the ones most able to come up with an upfront payment and have a better shot at getting placement at retail. In fact, the only way a small company is going to be able to be involved in a large movie is through a sub-licensing agreement.

Longstanding relationships between companies and studios also factor into the decision, as does a desire on the part of the studios to avoid conflicts within a company.

In the current market, toy deals are typically signed early on in the movie development process. The toy companies, which once labored in a semi-vacuum replicating what the studio gave them, now have a place at the table during development, and plot points, vehicles and other components of a movie are often considered for their toyetic (to use a bit of industry jargon) appeal.

Toys, as noted above, are determined by the plot of the movie, the characters, and the play potential. But they also have to be considered within the context of the entire licensing program. For instance, many movies have historically had fast food promotions as well, and care needs to be taken that the free toy at a fast food restaurant doesn't cannibalize the toy sales. (Particularly for young children and movies, the timeframe for playing with a toy is fairly short, and parents often feel that if they get that with a restaurant meal there is no need to buy a more expensive toy.)

Add to this the narrow retail opportunity. Toys for movies hit the shelves about 6 weeks before the premiere—about the time that all of the marketing effort is ramping up. The toys, however, like the movie, have to have strong sales right out of the box. The window is anywhere from 2-to-6 weeks for toys to find an audience.

This can be different with franchises, such as Batman, Spider-Man, Transformers, Avengers and so forth. These have become evergreen properties that sell even in a year when there is not a major movie release, another way of minimizing risk.

## *Television Shows*

In the contemporary market, there is more of an emphasis on television properties for action figures and other licensed properties. These properties that come into the home 5 days a week on television have a greater chance of developing and maintaining an audience—and an audience that will want to play with these characters.

The current dominance of Cartoon Network and Nickelodeon and newer channels like Disney Junior provide a 24/7 platform for kids to engage with a character. The shows become one of the most effective marketing tools for the properties and can drive kids's awareness and preferences more predictably than virtually any other medium. These platforms provide the opportunity to build a franchise over time, an essential component of the marketing process.

Of course not every property has the benefit of this level of exposure, and so an analysis of these properties in the early stages must take that into account. Chances are if you're the 4th or 5th most popular license within a demographic, it's not going to become a major hit, though if carefully managed in terms of product and distribution, it can attract a niche audience.

## *Brands*

Brands in the toy business have been effective for differentiating product. In toy cars, such as Hot Wheels and Matchbox, the number of licenses on a single car can be mind-boggling, particularly if it's a racecar that has a lot of corporate logos on it. Each of those requires a separate licensing agreement with the property holder. Names such as John Deere and Caterpillar are effective in differentiating toy trucks, tractors and construction equipment. In this case, the purchase decision is usually made at point-of-sale, and purchasers are more likely to go with the recognized name, even when there's a slight price differential because it more clearly replicates what children see in their world.

The question a licensee always needs to ask in considering taking on a brand is whether or not it adds an important level of realism to a toy or provides enough of a marketing hook.

For instance, food-making products while never blockbusters do have a decent position in the activity aisle. Does adding the brands Slurpee, Icee, Betty Crocker or Taco Bell (all of which have been used) add enough value and sales potential to offset the incremental costs of using a license? Certainly in a category where the volume of television licensing can be less than others, the license creates a difference at point of sale.

### *Licensing Out*

Toy companies that have established brands can also license those to manufacturers in other categories. The number of brands that are viable licenses are relatively few. Barbie, Hot Wheels, My Little Pony and Transformers are just four examples. Mattel and Hasbro can generate additional revenue through licensing programs, largely.

### *A Few Final Words About Licensing*

This discussion only scratches the surface of this complex and diverse business. The Licensing Industries Merchandisers' Association likes to talk about the licensing process as an industry, and it holds a trade show every year to showcase licenses. However, like the movie business, since every deal is different and every product performs differently, it's hard to quantify this as an industry.

Moreover, given the unpredictable nature of the business, and its high-risk nature, it is often characterized as one that's selling "fairy dust," particularly when it comes to entertainment properties. Like other areas of the toy industry, there is a great dependence on a gut feel, and over years it's possible to develop a level of experience and engage in the kind of analysis that will somewhat mitigate risk. Still, what looks like a sure thing can fail, and what no one thought about can become a major hit.

It's questionable whether there is really the time to do the kind of analysis that, say, a consumer package goods company might do prior to launching a product, so very often licensing decisions are made on a gut instinct. For example, no one thought "Toy Story" would be a good movie for licensing, so a small company called Thinkway made some toys, and it's been a steady producer for nearly two decades. At the same time, some movies do really well at the box office and don't have toys attached. When the sequel comes along, people think, "Well, if it *had* had toys, they would have done well." (That was the case with "Shrek," and the toys tanked. Not every movie lends itself to a viable toy program.) When and if they don't, everyone is surprised. In other businesses, no one would take this kind of risk. In toys, they do, and it can be a spectacular success or a crash-and-burn failure. The hope is that enough work so that it can mitigate losses.

*Television Advertising*

There is still no tactic as effective for driving broad-based awareness and reaching a target audience of children than television advertising. From the 1950s through the end of the 20th century, it was the only way, as few channels broadcasting children's television at specific times virtually assured an audience. Today, the market is fragmented with many different channels targeting different demographics. On the one hand, that's made it easier to target ads against specific groups based on viewer profiles. On the other, it's hard to know where to put the advertising.

Add to this the growth of DVR recording, time-shifting, on-demand, video, streaming media and the increasing move away from either broadcast or cable TV and you've got a market that is in flux. The primary consideration, though, is that individual consumers have become their own programmers. A parent can pretty much choose what his or her child watches and when, and with the rise of internet-connected TVs, avoiding commercials is easier to do than ever.

That's where hit shows come in. The two major networks for children's TV advertising in the current market are Nickelodeon and Cartoon Network. With shows kids watch, this is where toymakers are concentrating the majority of their TV dollars. Disney has become a player with its wholly owned cable channels such as Disney XD, and while still small, Hasbro's channel, The Hub, has been making some progress. (Interestingly, toymakers are resistant to advertising on The Hub, as they don't want to be funneling revenue to Hasbro.)

Another challenge with TV advertising is the timing. The toy industry is really one of the only industries where a product that is first seen in March or April is being advertised on television in the Fourth Quarter. Other businesses simply don't work quite that way. It makes research and testing virtually impossible with respect to messages, executions and so forth, other than in terms of preference testing. Whereas a large consumer product company might put several versions of a commercial or a strategy in to focus groups, there simply isn't the time to do that in the toy industry.

And speaking of timing, most of the prime TV advertising time for the fourth quarter is purchased in the first part of the year. Manufacturers are asked to make commitments to TV budgets when they haven't finalized the product or the sales. For larger companies who commit to time, it's easy to change products, but not so easy for smaller companies.

Part of the solution to this is to design features into the toy that are specifically TV demonstrable. This is why marketing departments get involved with a toy early on in the process. A good toy commercial shows, on average, three features in 30 seconds, and it needs to be eye-catching. As discussed earlier, the motion in Tickle Me Elmo was added in the marketing process to give it a feature that would play on TV. On the flip side of this, there is also the issue of toys that are over-designed. When the commercial is going to show only three things, and be sold on the basis of those things, does it need to do 10 or 12? Perhaps not for a feature plush toy or a mechanical toy. Perhaps so for an educational toy. This is very situation/product dependent.

At the same time, some toys and toy categories aren't very TV-friendly. It's difficult to advertise games on TV, for instance, unless it's a so-called Skill-and-Action game that has visual, demonstrable features. (Hasbro had a lot of success in promoting "Family Game Night" on TV, but that also promoted games overall, and was a boon to competing manufacturers.)

Companies are, rightly, very sensitive about the costs related to television advertising. It's not just the expense of buying time but the cost of commercial production that has been growing in recent years. However, it's possible to produce a toy commercial relatively inexpensively, compared to some others, say for pharmaceuticals. Usually shot on one set or with one series of shots and often done in Canada where costs are much lower for U.S. manufacturers, the point of the commercial is always to make the toy the star. But, and here we go again, what one spends on a TV ad is going to be dependent on the toy, the market and a variety of factors. One of the largest, however, is the total budget. With an advertising budget of only $1 MM, it's not practical to spend 15% of that on the production of a TV commercial. Rather, it's better to create an exciting commercial on a shoestring budget and spend the rest of the money on buying TV time. It's also important to note that children are not as visually sophisticated as adults, so the production values of a toy commercial don't need to be the same as those of a luxury car. There are advertising agencies that specialize in these types of commercials, as well as buying services that can help create the best ad buy across the board.

If children are not visually sophisticated, they are, however, highly impressionable. Since Peggy Charren created Action for Children's Television in 1968, marketing to children has been a volatile topic. Organizations such as The Campaign for a Commercial-Free Childhood advocate a zero-tolerance approach to marketing targeted to children. While it has some adherents, it has yet to make significant inroads into the marketing business. While parents are concerned about the amount of screen time children have, the vast majority would not agree with the almost total banning of it. ("Screen Time" has replaced TV watching as the number of screens children use for entertainment has proliferated.)

The legislation that covers advertising to children was first past in 1990 and is still in effect. Enforcement falls under the Federal Communications Commission (FCC), and it covers networks, local broadcasters, and cable operators.

Among its provisions are that for programming intended for children age 12 and under, no more than 10.5 minutes per hour may be shown on weekends and 12 minutes per hour on weekdays. For children ages 16 and under, the FCC considers the amount of educational programming, requiring 3 hours of a week of such programming. License renewal is dependent on broadcasters meeting this number, though what is considered educational has been quite loosely interpreted.

A subsequent ruling by the FCC stated that shows based on a toy or product could not have advertising for that product within the show, though it could run following the show. For example, a cartoon show about Batman could not have commercials for Batman toys within it.

In addition to the law, the advertising business in the United States is self-regulating, unlike many other countries. The Children's Advertising Review Unit (CARU) established in 1974 has published guidelines, and it reviews advertising to make sure that it's not misleading, makes unrealistic promises or shows toys in ways that they could not appear in normal play. (Baby Boomers, for instance grew up hearing, "PF Flyers make you run faster and jump higher." Such a claim would not be made today. In addition, a toy plane might be shown to fly independently when it does not, and CARU would require that the commercial show the child's hand.) CARU works with manufacturers to try to get voluntary cooperation with the guidelines.

Broadcasters also maintain advertising review units designed to ensure that all television advertising meets mandatory and voluntary standards.

### A Few Final Words About TV Advertising

Just as TV advertising has remained the number one awareness driver among kids, despite all the challenges of a dynamic market, it is not as effective with parents. In the current market, a parent is more likely to do research online, rather than wait for a TV commercial to come on. The exception, of course, have been educational toys and toys marketed for children under two where the parents or caregivers are the ones making the purchasing decisions. Yet as more and more parents go online, marketers are in many cases diverting that money to the more economical online advertising and promotion, which we'll discuss in a moment.

In addition to reaching children, TV advertising serves one more important function in the overall toy marketing process. Retailers demand it. Part of the sales process is showing an advertising and marketing schedule that includes TV advertising. Forget about the fact that what's shown in sales meetings in the early part of the year often bears no resemblance to what happens in Q4, TV advertising remains critical to buyers because they see it works.

Simply put, when toys are advertised on television they sell more. Now, this often leads manufacturers to heavy up on advertising during the early days of a release since those first weeks on the shelf are critical to retailers' ongoing commitment only to pull back later, but that's a gamble that sometimes works and sometimes doesn't. The hope is that the early advertising-driven sales will create enough momentum that other less expensive marketing tactics will be able to maintain that momentum. A typical advertising schedule may play ads in heavy rotation early on and then return to a heavy rotation in the weeks leading up to the holidays. When it works, this keeps sales high, or at acceptable levels, throughout. When it doesn't, sales fall off as advertising is withdrawn.

There's not great science or mystery to this. With so many things competing for children's attention and with their tastes and wants so changeable, being top-of-mind is critically important.

## Online

Talk to people who specialize in television advertising, and they'll tell you that Internet advertising doesn't work. Talk to people who sell online advertising, and they'll tell you you're wasting your money on TV. No big surprise there.

The truth, however, is, as usual, somewhat more in the middle. However, the same issues apply as choosing where to air TV commercials. (And, indeed, the booming household penetration of high-speed Internet has made it possible to put TV-style commercials online.) One of the great things about online advertising, however, is that it's easily quantifiable as views, click-throughs and more can be tabulated on a daily basis so that advertising can be adjusted based on responses.

Traditional advertising, however, is only one use of the Internet in the marketing process. In fact, the online world is also evolving so quickly that staying on top of it requires constant attention. Any toymaker, retailer, inventor or marketer that fails to get a grip on the way the online world is affecting the toy market might as well hang it up. That's not too blunt a statement. As more and more shopping moves online, as technology drives the information gathering, shopping and purchasing processes, online has to some extent leveled the playing field but it also puts new demands on a business that is highly entrenched in "the way we've always done it," and, especially among larger companies, can be slow to adapt.

While online marketing is the subject of its own studies and a discipline unto itself, there are some key elements that contribute to the effective use of online for toy marketing.

## Content is King

This will be familiar to students of any industry and online in the current marketplace. The majority of toy buyers in the United States are moms, ages 22–36, and they are getting their information online. They routinely turn to online sources for information about any purchase. When a kid says he or she wants something is online. Moreover, these consumers were raised to be skeptical of, and sensitive to, traditional advertising. As a result the rise of the mom bloggers, independent review sites and peer reviews on online retailers, are critical. These moms are looking for information they can relate to from sources they trust, and that's not necessarily manufacturer or traditional advertising. What has emerged is a more educated consumer than we have seen previously and a marketplace where with very few exceptions—toys bought on impulse at point-of-sale being one—purchases are researched more carefully than ever before. Peer reviews, in particular, or independent sites with a track record of providing good information are especially trusted. Less trusted are reviews on retailing sites that have clearly been written by the marketing people and posted from home computers or sites from manufacturers targeted to moms and toy purchasers.

For kids, virtually every toy for children ages 4 and up has some sort of online presence. This is a way to deepen the online relationship between the child and the brand. Toys such as Webkinz that were linked to the Internet, or entertainment sites like Club Penguin compete for traditional toy dollars, but companies like LEGO use their online presence to drive storylines for some of its properties as entertainment.

Kids raised in this digital age are also very discerning customers. Sites have to be engaging, intuitive and relevant to them. They can't simply be advertisements for a toy or property. The entertainment must be sophisticated and competitive with other types of sites they are consuming. Too often companies try to save money by creating sites with functionality that's too limited and as a result lose their audience. Sites like those for Cartoon Network, Nickelodeon and Disney are where kids are spending their time, and if they're bored, new stimulation is a click away. Thus, careful analysis of an online strategy is critical—for all audiences to be sure, but especially for children.

Any online material targeted to children must be what's called COPPA-compliant, that is must comply with the Children's Online Privacy act that's designed to protect children online. This covers things like not collecting personally identifiable information about children and often requires parental consent for children, and the act defines children as anyone under the age of 13.

Creating relevant content for target audiences is essential, particularly as more and more families and children are spending less time watching television and more time-consuming information online. More and more kids are going online, and they have a wide variety of choices, so creating a site for kids that is engaging and "sticky" is essential for building engagement with and demand for a given product.

## LEGO: Online as a Prime Entertainment Source

In recent years, LEGO has posted impressive growth every year as it has broadened its audience, moving beyond basis construction and into narrative-based play. The company has never abandoned its core consumer, which is a kid (or adult) who loves building, but they've also added a variety of intellectual properties (IP) to their portfolio that have spurred this growth.

Traditionally, construction play has encompassed three components: build, play and display. LEGO has emphasized the play component over the passive display and in the process created deeper engagement among its consumers.

The recent introduction of Ninjago, a story-based, Asian-inspired world of intrigue and adventure, has been driven both through exciting building sets and an online experience. The complex story has come to life through a series of animated webisodes and the Ninjago site has become a destination for its fans. Thus, while attracting new fans, the company uses the online entertainment to deepen the relationship with the existing fans and drive more sales of its product.

This has become a highly effective way to reach a niche market, and for the fans of the story and the product, the site becomes a destination for the consumption of entertainment that, for this group, replaces television watching.

The company is launching new IP with the same strategy, and more and more companies are looking to the online space to speak directly to its core consumers.

Certainly as online entertainment continues to evolve, what is emerging and will continue to emerge is a kind of narrow-casting that allows companies to speak directly to its core consumers at a cost significantly below the costs of TV production, while concentrating on attracting new consumers to a property.

### *Driving Traffic is Still Important*

Like toys, even the best web sites are worthless unless someone finds them.

There are a variety of different advertising options on related sites, though at least in the toy industry, the traditional banner advertising is giving way to more intrusive pop-ups, video and wallpaper advertising. As consumers get more and more adept at ignoring the banner ads, finding new ways to grab attention online is pushing innovation in advertising.

Including sites on toys both for customer service and engagement with a property is important. Any traditional advertising should be tagged with a web site, and of course, any content should drive traffic back to your site. (Content is covered in the following section on public relations.)

By far the most traffic generated in the toy industry is through search, at least for potential consumers. Parents go online to get information they need, and you can bet that if it's about a toy a small child in particular has requested, that search is going to be somewhat challenging. A strong SEO (search engine optimization) program is critical to helping products be found online, and investment in this is critical—and too often overlooked.

## A Few Final Words About Online

If you're going to be in the toy industry, you must be online, that's the simple truth. And getting attention online is as competitive as within the industry. This requires investment in strategy and execution that's going to result in effective outreach.

Interestingly, in recent years, many companies, even larger ones, have downplayed the importance of online, largely because retailers have focused on TV advertising commitments from toymakers as essential to their purchasing decisions. As the understanding grows of the role that online plays in the overall marketing mix, retailers are also considering those strategies, particularly as more and more sales move online. As noted, in 2012, approximately 10% of toy sales in the United States were online, and that number is only continuing to grow.

For marketers, online is also relatively easy to test and costs a fraction of television advertising. The current trend is to allocate a small percentage of the TV budget into structured online tests. The advantage of online is also that it's completely measurable and very flexible, which allows it to be adjusted on the fly—perfect for the dynamic nature of the toy industry.

The other major advantage of online marketing is the ability to target a message precisely to a specific audience. The market, as discussed, may indeed be fragmented, but in the case of online marketing that fragmentation can work to the advantage of marketers. For instance, a targeted soft launch (a launch that is done quietly without promotion beyond the sites selected) can gauge the response of an audience in a way that can be extrapolated to the larger population. This both controls spending up front and minimizes risk if something doesn't hit. The challenge is finding exactly the right places to go to target the audience and then developing and implementing a communication strategy that effectively communicates the product and, hopefully, drives sales.

## Public Relations

Public relations has played a central role in toy marketing for many years. In the early 1960s, publicists helped establish LEGO in the United States through events, participation in television shows, and on through the great games boom in the 1980s, PR was the primary marketing tactic used to drive both awareness and purchase.

Categories like board games have always been more responsive to PR than TV advertising, and PR has effectively been used to get news coverage for toys and drive grassroots awareness.

Linda Pezzano, mentioned earlier who was the mastermind behind the launches of Trivial Pursuit and Pictionary, knew the advantage of the one-on-one recommendations of friends and the power of a network whether accessed in person or through the media to drive consumer awareness. Like others in the business, her goal was always to get the "third party endorsement" of editors, celebrities, or other influencers that would get the toy buying public to pay attention.

The practice of PR in the toy industry has changed radically in recent years due to the rise of social media, such as Twitter, Facebook Instagram and other social media platforms. While placement on television shows still delivers a lot of impact, the real work of PR in the current toy market is to try to leverage the high profile appearances with steady information about products and, most importantly, customer engagement.

The fragmentation of the media marketplace that has affected television advertising has had a similar impact on PR. Today's PR professionals need to know social media intimately, including mommy bloggers (some of them paid as "Brand Ambassadors" or some such title), Facebook pages, Twitter accounts, Pinterest pages, and many more. The objective is still to engage as much of a target audience as possible in as many ways as possible, but for today's toy buyers that is done primarily online.

The principal impact all of this has had is to give rise to a world where everyone can be an expert. Forget the fact that a blogger with a sample of her child is not what any researcher would call valid or even representative of anything larger than that child's, the current media has created a plethora of experts, both credited and uncredited. In today's crowded media market, an individual opinion can be spun as expertise, and anyone with a computer can have a communications platform. The barrier to entry is so low that virtually anyone with a keyboard and an ability to get samples can present themselves as an expert. More and more, however, companies inundated by requests for samples have had to do their homework to determine what media outlets to work with, what their audiences are and their reach. Fortunately, these data are all easily available. A fallout in the blogging community has already begun as fewer and fewer independent bloggers are able to monetize their efforts, which requires building a sufficient audience and traffic so that companies will want to target them. After a few years in which the novelty of the so-called blogosphere was attracting all kinds of attention, PR professionals are doing more careful research before committing time, energy, and samples to bloggers. The upside is that the bloggers who are emerging as the leaders with strong voices and loyal communities are becoming an exceptional asset in PR efforts, taking up the space that has been lost by the decline in consumer magazines and their aging demographic.

Most large companies have internal PR teams, and many smaller companies work with agencies that specialize in the toy industry. Again, PR has been downplayed in some companies because retailers made purchases based on TV advertising and not other marketing tactics. However, as the evidence that an engaged community becomes more and more effective at driving sales, thanks to the data collecting capabilities of online activity, that is beginning to shift as well.

Still, PR is still often then less-loved stepchild in many toy companies. Old habits die hard, and so you'll still see companies spending huge amounts on large, one-day events designed to be brand building when an online contest may actually sell more product for a fraction of the cost.

But PR is not merely about driving sales. For publicly traded companies, investor relations is part of the job, targeting Wall Street analysts as a critically important constituency. As we'll see in the next chapter, many of these analysts struggle to grasp the nature of the toy business and the ways in which it differs from other industries they track.

Part of an effective PR program in today's market is that it engages consumers in a dialogue. Facebook pages that invite consumers to post pictures and make comments unfiltered (with the exception of profanity or anything that would violate terms of service) allows consumers to trust a brand and feel engaged with it. One need only look at the number of fans and interactions that brands like Play-Doh, NERF or LeapFrog have online to see that their consumers are deeply engaged in the brand. Again, as noted earlier, with more and more research being done by consumers before purchase and with a demand for more information, the PR function has become more and more about highly targeted communications. Today's consumers expect companies to engage with them, and those that they perceive engage in an authentic and relevant way are more likely to generate positive impressions and brand loyalty.

PR, of course, can cut both ways. The toy industry is also what we often call a "lighting rod" industry. However far-fetched, the toy industry always makes good copy for presumably scandalous and sensational news coverage. We're not talking here about situations like the lead paint issues that occurred in 2007. More, we're talking about the kind of issues where someone gets it in their head that a talking stuffed toy is cursing or that a doll is somehow affecting a child's self-image or fostering a specific role. Forget that these are adult projections onto what are essentially inert pieces of plastic, the totemic power of toys, and the presumption that a conspiracy is behind it is something that is featured in the news with great regularity. It makes a good story, whether or not it's true, and managing that kind of situation falls under the responsibilities of the PR department.

PR budgets, as you might have guessed, vary widely based on the product, though they are comparatively small related to advertising budgets. PR agencies generally work on retainers that can range from about $7,500 per month for a single program from a small agency to $20,000 or more per month for large-scale brand initiatives.

### *A Few Final Words About Public Relations*

The rise of online has had one major impact on the practice of PR—not just in the toy industry. Online has made results measurable on a much more granular level. Whereas what the best PR departments could do in the past was to record audience numbers and demonstrate reach and frequency, it was impossible to isolate the performance of any individual piece or the overall performance of an initiative. With online, it's possible to measure the impact of a blog post by the number of clicks form a specific post, putting hard numbers to something that was previously more amorphous.

In addition, depending on how a program is structured, it could even be possible to track clicks to a retailer and then figure out the conversion rate. That is, the percentage of people who came through a specific online source and proceeded all the way to a sale. This would not control for other influences or whether someone clicked through to something and later bought, but for at least one step, there are numbers available that weren't before. What this may facilitate for creative PR people is structuring different messages to see how they perform and affect behavior.

Like so many other aspects of the toy industry, this is one that is changing as the media marketplace changes, but what's constant is the need to communicate and engage consumers to generate awareness, belief, purchase and, in a perfect world, advocacy.

## CHAPTER 6

# The Money Game: The Financial Realities of the Toy Industry

By now, it should come as no surprise that the financial structure of the toy industry is unique and uniquely challenging.

The primary—and somewhat obvious—reason for this is that approximately 50% of the year's retail sales are made in the fourth Quarter, with the bulk of those (as much as 25% of the year's total sales) coming in December. Not to be overly dramatic, but 2 years of effort, planning and expense face a make-or-break 20 days at the end of the year.

Ranking toy companies is never an easy task. Privately held toy companies like MGA Entertainment do not have to report their sales, and there are many conglomerates like Disney, which generates only part of its revenue from toy sales and licensing. Similarly, VTECH which is also in the phone and electronic business does derive part of its revenue from toy sales, as does Bandai, but these companies do not break out the specific contribution of toys to their overall performance.

Traditional, publicly traded, toy companies in the United States ranked by revenue for 2012 are

1. Mattel—$6.42 B
2. Hasbro—$4.19B
3. LEGO—$4.04 B
4. Jakks Pacific—$666. 8 MM
5. LeapFrog—$581.3 MM
6. Mega Bloks—$420.3 MM

These are what would be considered the top tier toy companies. The second tier and below are all smaller companies, and of the approximately 600 toy companies in the United. States and their revenues are wide ranging. Companies in the top 25 might have revenues of $150MM, while there are many in the $20–$25MM range, and even some companies that are profitable on revenues of $5–$10 MM. It varies by product and, of course, the make-up and objectives of the specific company.

This concentration of a few companies in the top tier is the result of a variety of factors, largely acquisitions. Of these six, LEGO is the only one that has not grown through acquisition over the years. They've done it solely on the basis of expanding product.

During the mid-1960s and 1970s, the overall trend of corporations diversifying their holdings inspired many major corporations to get into the toy industry. The toy companies, many of which had been family businesses, were only too willing to cash out. What followed was a massive absorption and consolidation of small companies that lasted until the early 1980s. What the major corporations had not anticipated was that the nature of the toy business would end up being a drag on the balance sheet for three quarters of the year, with the hope of making it up with all-important holiday sales.

Here are just a few examples of how companies were bought, sold, combined, and reconfigured over the years as names that Baby Boomers recall with great affection became part of larger companies that focused on toys.

CBS, the broadcaster, got into the toy business in 1966 with the acquisition of Creative Playthings, a company that made wooden preschool toys. The rationale, as the story goes, was that founder William Paley's wife liked the products, so Paley bought the company. CBS would later acquire Gabriel Toys, educational toymaker Child Guidance, swingset maker Gym-Dandy, spring horse maker Wonder Products, and one of the biggest toy companies of the 1950s and 1960s, Ideal. In 1985, as Laurence Tisch began controlling CBS, he began the process of divesting the corporation of the companies it had bought (which also included Steinway Pianos and Fender Guitars among others) and focus on its core businesses. Creative Playthings had become a brand of wooden playground equipment by that time, and it was sold to a company in Framingham, MA. Jakks Pacific ultimately acquired Child Guidance, and the Ideal brand is currently being revived by Poof-Slinky. For the most part, as we'll see in a moment, different toy companies cherry-picked the assets of the companies as they were shutting down.

Hasbro also grew steadily through acquisition. Founded in 1923, the company had been known primarily for school supplies—at least until it debuted Mr. Potato Head in 1952. Hasbro began acquiring toy companies in earnest in the mid 1980s. In 1984, Hasbro bought Milton Bradley, which had previously acquired Playskool in 1968. General Mills, the cereal company, had acquired classic game maker Parker Brothers in 1968, later combining it with Kenner Toys. These were combined as Kenner Parker toys and sold to Tonka in 1987. Hasbro picked them all up in 1991. Hasbro acquired Avalon Hill Games in 1998, which had previously absorbed 3M games in 1976. Hasbro also acquired Tiger Electronics and Galoob toys in 1998. Wizards of the Coast had acquired TSR, makers of Dungeons & Dragons in 1997, and Hasbro picked them up in 1999. Hasbro's most recent acquisition was the game company Cranium in 2008.

Jakks Pacific has grown primarily through acquisitions over its relatively short history. Founded in 1995, 2 years later it acquired Remco, Child Guidance and carmaker Road Champions. In 2002, it acquired Toymax and Go Fly a Kite. A year later, it acquired Trendmasters, and in 2004, it acquired Play Along Toys. In 2008, it acquired Kids Only Toys, dollmaker Tollytots and costume maker Disguise. Throughout the years, it acquired a variety of other related companies expanding into the pet and stationery businesses.

Mattel, too, has had its share of acquisitions, though not quite as many as Hasbro. Founded in 1945, Mattel had originally made picture frames with a smaller business in dollhouse furniture. Two years later, it began making musical toys including the Uke-A-Doodle and Jack in the Boxes. In 1995, the company teamed up with "The Mickey Mouse Club" and also began making the cap pistols that Baby Boomers craved. Of course, Barbie followed in 1959, and the company never made a picture frame again. Over the years, the company made many hit toys, but it didn't start acquisitions until 1986, when it purchased ARCO Toys. In 1988, it purchased upscale dollmaker Corolle. In 1989, it acquired die-cast car maker Corgi. In 1991, it bought Aviva Sports and a year later International Games. In 1993, Mattel acquired Fisher-Price, which had been owned by Quaker Oats from 1967 to 1991, when the company became independent. In 1997, the company acquired Tyco and with it the Sesame Street name and Matchbox, the latter having been acquired by Tyco in 1992. In 1998, the company bought the British company Bluebird Toys and with it the popular Polly Pocket Brand. A year later, it acquired The Learning Company in a move that turned out to be a mistake as educational software wasn't part of the company's expertise. Mattel would divest itself of different brands over the years as well as it continued to focus on its core businesses. Mattel's most recent acquisition in 2012 was for HIT Entertainment, producers of the popular series Thomas The Tank Engine. This gave the company a foothold in the entertainment business and more importantly ownership of Thomas, which it had previously licensed and for which it will now receive the revenues from Thomas licensees all over the world.

No one will blame you if your head is reeling from all of this. There were several reasons for all these acquisitions. First, now that the companies were publicly traded, one of the surest ways of demonstrating growth was through acquisition. Second, as the toy industry became more and more international, the assets of the companies acquired included factories, international subsidiaries, and broader opportunities for distribution.

Also not surprising is that the rate of acquisitions in recent years has slowed considerably. One can certainly ask, who is there to acquire, but there are still deals being done. In 2013, Propel Equity Partners acquired arts-and-crafts company Alex, having previously acquired small game company Fundex and Poof-Slinky. As with the first boom of acquisitions in the 1960s, these were small, privately held companies, and it was a good deal for the principals.

Far more common in today's market is the acquisition of certain assets, brands, or products. A major company is far more likely to acquire a brand or an item from a small company in order to give it wider, mass-market distribution rather than the entire company with all its potential liabilities.

Similar consolidations have happened in the retail sector, though not as much by acquisition. In the years after World War II sales were concentrated locally major department stores. Of course, there was FAO Schwarz, which was already an institution and did a huge mail order catalog business and Kay-Bee toys, which had been founded in 1922. Toys "R" Us was founded in 1948 to be a "toy supermarket." This was perfect for the Eisenhower years, and later in the early 1960s, Lionel Leisure and Kiddie City Stores sprung up as well. Woolworth's, Kresges and Sears were all major players in the category as well, and many Baby Boomers remember growing up with the Sears Wish Book and plotting what they would be putting on the lists for Santa.

From the 1970s to the 1990s, retail in general was consolidated as large conglomerates bought local stores and that included toy stores. Toys "R" Us was effectively a category killer. From the 1960s on, the company bought smaller, regional toy chains and consolidated them under the Toys "R" Us banner. Given its size, it was able to continue to sell toys at a discount, undercutting department stores who eventually got out of the business. But Toys "R" Us, which had gone public in 1978, would get a taste of its own medicine as booming retailers Wal-Mart and Target were undercutting Toys "R" Us on price and taking a significant share of the business. In 2005, Toys "R" Us was bought by a private equity group consisting of Kolberg Kravis Roberts & Co, Vornado Realty Trust, and Bain Capital Partners in a leveraged buyout. Recent plans for an IPO did not come off after Toys "R" Us had a challenging year in 2011.

Today, the toy retail market, as noted is dominated by Wal-Mart, Target, Toys "R" Us, and Amazon. Wal-Mart and Target are likely to carry only the most in-demand and promoted items in a given year—perhaps 1,200 different items. Toys "R" Us, on the other hand may carry as many as 7,000 different items. Wal-Mart and Target do have an advantage in that they can offer popular toys at deep discounts as a way of driving traffic into the stores. Any profit they give up, they hope to make up on other items consumers purchase while in the store. This is generally referred to as a "market basket play," as the Wal-Mart and Target are more concerned about the gross margins of the entire purchase rather than just an individual item. Amazon, on the other hand, is valued on its revenue per visitor, a version of the market basket play, rather than on the profitability of an individual toy. So, it, too, can undercut Toys "R" Us on price. What this has left Toys "R" Us with is a strategy for being in stock on key items when other stores have sold through their allocation.

And then there's the consumer buying patterns. In recent years, retailers have taken early markdowns on products in October and November, sometimes drastically. What this has done is condition shoppers to wait until the last minute—sometimes the last weekend before Christmas—to buy toys because of anticipated sales. (The exceptions of course are so-called hot items that may be sold out.)

These unplanned markdowns can be a cause of contention between manufacturers and retailers as retailers may request discounts or markdown allowances that haven't been planned. This is what we mean when we say that no two deals are the same, and no sale is final until it is. The negotiation, according to people involved in the process, is almost never ending. And right after the holidays, the next year kicks into high gear.

From a manufacturers' perspective, the toy industry remains a capital-intensive business, and, as should be perfectly clear by now, it's one for which there are no consistent business models or formulas for success. Essentially, a large company like a Mattel or Hasbro will have to invest for 18 months or more before they begin to know whether or not their investment is going to pay off. That window is slightly smaller for a mid-size company, and for small, independent companies, that window can be a year or less. Still the costs for design, molds, samples, packaging, shipping, sales, and so forth are all allocated and spent before the first reads on sales are available.

For companies like Mattel and Hasbro, sales across a portfolio of products generate the revenue that allows them to invest in research and development. In recent years, the emphasis within these companies has been on looking for acquisition targets that will expand a portfolio both to enhance retail relationships and how the company is viewed in the investment community. Thus, for Hasbro, there has been a solid expansion of the NERF brand, which now incorporates Super Soakers, which were previously sold individually. In most cases, this has little or no impact at the consumer level where decisions are still made on the basis of individual products rather than buying more deeply in a brand. There is some evidence from our conversations with consumers that the solid equity of the NERF brand to consumers has married well with the Super Soaker brand. Conversely, the move to merge all Hasbro word games under the Scrabble brand was confusing, a move that Hasbro has since backed away from. Mattel's standard portfolio includes Barbie, Hot Wheels and other brands. While there are inevitable fluctuations from year to year, these core businesses are essential to providing a relatively stable foundation for new introductions and expansion.

For smaller companies, particularly independent and start-ups, raising money can be very hard. For many years, smaller companies used factors, companies that purchased accounts receivable for 75–85% of the total, which gave companies the cash flow they needed to function throughout the year. This minimized certain amounts of risk by transferring ownership to the factor, but it was expensive. Today, it's far more common to have investors with an ownership stake in a company or for a company to be in partnership with a manufacturing concern or other partners to reduce up front costs.

Still, as many small toy companies will attest, finding these partnerships or raising money is not necessarily easy in a world where sophisticated investors are looking for proven business models or categories of goods that have consistent performance, rather than taking a gamble on an item or two that is wholly dependent, as we've said before, on the whims of a child. Essentially what toy companies are asking potential investors to do is to buy into a vision and creativity, and to a certain extent, the track record of the people involved. In this way, the toy industry is more closely analogous to the entertainment business, where investors are asked to invest in a concept. Particularly when a concept is new and hasn't been tried before, this is where the "gut instinct" comes into play. But, as with show business, only a percentage of the toys introduced become profitable and fewer become long-term sellers, so anyone investing in the toy industry should only be playing with money they can afford to lose.

At the same time, as discussed earlier, many established toy companies are shifting the costs of research and development and even initial production to smaller companies, acquiring products from distribution, or working with inventors. Both of these are significant ways of reducing risk.

With respect to public versus private ownership, it's almost always better for toy companies be privately owned. It's much easier for a private company to weather the cyclical nature of the business rather than being held to account by shareholders and Wall Street for the quarter when performance is going to be down. In the early 1970s, as many large corporations sought to expand and diversify, they bought up toy companies. CBS, Inc. ultimately acquired five, only to divest itself of them in the mid-1980s when the toy company's natural performance created a drag on the overall numbers that wasn't always wholly offset by one quarter of strong sales.

The reasons to go public are the same as in any other business—to raise capital for expansion or for owners to cash out. With the latter, it's much more likely for a company to try to cash out through going public when private equity has been funding the company. In this scenario, a company that may be underperforming is bought out by a private equity firm, returned to a strong level of performance and then off-loaded through going public. The unique challenge of the toy industry is that because this is a product-driven business, a company can be streamlined, downsized and made attractive on paper, but at the end of the day, one hit product or one major failure can change the entire financial picture for a company. This tends to make investors wary, again because there are few accurate predictors of success over time.

For publicly traded companies, the stock price sometimes reflects current sales, but more often is a gamble on the future. The best investment analysts look not just at the current numbers but the larger cultural impact of what's driving them. Whether it's the broader-based popular culture, research with suppliers or drilling down into the fundamental performance of the business, analysts come up with a buy or sell recommendation based on the stock price. And, analysts can be as right or wrong as anyone else when dealing with the unknowable—such as how a movie or TV show is going to perform and whether it has been translated into toys that children will love—and children are notoriously oblivious of the effects of their whims on stock prices. Certainly in talking with analysts over the years, they do put a lot of emphasis on how the product portfolios mentioned above perform. This is perceived as the core business, and for many years, for example, the valuation of Mattel was based primarily on the performance of Barbie in the market. Providing ongoing analysis on publicly traded toy companies is a challenge. Since so much of the product is new every year, it's very difficult to determine whether a company is on the rise, is flat or declining. Moreover, stock prices don't always reflect current performance. The announcement of a license for a movie 2 years down the road may be sufficient to keep the stock price up because of anticipation that toys from the movie will do well. This can happen even if the sales in the current year are lagging. This is the case when the investment is a longer-term play, and as one analyst who asked not to be named said an investment bank has a great deal of money that they have to put somewhere, so the job is to find places where they can invest that will mitigate risk and have potential for growth. Still, understanding the changing nature of the toy industry provides unique challenges to investors and the investment community.

As with the products themselves, investing in the toy business will continue to be something that happens on an individualized basis and that isn't necessarily dependent on logic. In the private world, many people think they have the insight to know what's going to work. Sometimes they're even right. In the public world, toy stocks are more of a gamble, and the investments are made not so much on the individual toys but the track record of the company, its overall performance relative to expectations and predictions (commonly called "guidance") and knowledge of the industry in all its various and unpredictable guises.

# CHAPTER 7

# So You Still Want to Play?

Having made it this far and waded through all the complexities and caveats, if you still want to be in the toy business then you might just have the intestinal fortitude it demands. All kidding aside, there are many paths to a career in the toy industry. An undergraduate degree in business, marketing, or communications can be helpful, and an MBA is a requirement if you want to be an analyst. It doesn't hurt to have some experience in research and an understanding of product management and manufacturing.

If you want to be in design or development, you'll need an understanding of engineering, design, and marketing. There are two programs that specialize in toys—Otis College of Art and Design in Los Angeles and at The Fashion Institute of Technology in New York. Both of these programs have exceptional success at getting graduates placed in toy companies.

For either of these tracks you'll also need a working knowledge of child development, and an understanding of popular culture and sociology can't hurt. The nature of the toy business, as we've said, is that it reflects the culture, so your job is to find ways to reflect those trends in ways that are cognitively appropriate for the children you're intending them for.

And then there's coming up with your own ideas. This is more challenging than you might think. In fact, as noted earlier, it's about as easy to go into your room and write a hit screenplay as it is to create a successful toy. The fact of the matter is that more toys don't make it than do, and by make it we mean turn a profit. Still, toy companies rely on outside ideas. Most large toy companies have an inventor relations department that works with outside submissions. You'll probably need an agent or an alliance with a development company, however. You could work your heart out on building a model and designing a toy and send it in to a company only to have it returned unopened. It's not that you have a terrible idea.

Most companies have strict policies about accepting submissions and will tell you readily that they may be working on something that is similar. If you get so far as a meeting with a toy company, you may very well be asked to sign something acknowledging that they may have something in the works that is similar to what you're proposing. Since you can't trademark an idea, it's very difficult to protect your concept—this is something we discussed earlier, and what goes for toy companies is the same for individual inventors. If there are elements of your concept that can be patented, whether a design patent or a utility patent, it's best to have that at least in process before you start to shop your concept. Oh, and you should be aware that companies may also have people known as "patent breakers." These are engineers who are able to get around a patent and still have something perform a similar function. You're going to need a good lawyer if you decided to go it on your own.

Lest this seem too dark, companies value their relationship with the inventor community and are often in partnership with inventors who either make royalties on their creations or sell them outright. The relationship between inventors and toy companies can be very profitable for both, but to make it there, you'll need to build relationships and a track record.

Finally, you'll need to go through all the processes here to make sure your concept is viable. Remember, as we've said, the toy industry reflects the culture, so knowing where something has succeeded before or is established in the current adult culture is a key to creating something that will work in the toy industry. Given the number of toys that are introduced in any year, over time the number that have truly changed the industry are very few and far between.

Still, while there are many in the industry today who would warn you off it, this is still one of the most exciting, creative and engaging businesses you can be in. It can be a heck of a ride, but it's worth it to get to play all day every day (in a manner of speaking).

# EPILOGUE

# Play It Forward: Forecasting the Future

Telling the future of the toy industry has an accuracy rate that is probably on par with that of a street corner psychic. It's an industry whose doom is seen in every new technological innovation from television to the smartphone. It's an industry where new trends in education and entertainment are perceived to be a threat.

The fact of the matter is that none of these has materialized. Sure, technology has evolved at an almost-mind numbing pace. New modes of communication have changed how we interact and acquire information. But while this evolution has been fast, evolution of the human species is glacial in its speed. What this means is that the needs and benefits of play as an essential element of child development have remained virtually unchanged throughout the modern era. Boiled down, play serves three very basic functions for children: it provides new experiences, facilitates exploration of the world, and gives children a chance to express themselves.

The advent of new handheld electronics has, as mentioned earlier, only made the toybox bigger, as evidenced by the adoption of these technologies and the strong steady sales of basics such as construction and arts and crafts toys.

We do see a steady increase in costs, driven largely by changes in manufacturing and oil prices. The toy industry is a petroleum-dependent business, so the impact of those costs will be felt throughout the entire production and distribution channels.

Retailing will continue to move online, particularly for products that are kid-requested. The current 10-12% of annual toy sales online is steadily increasing every season as consumers do more research and shopping online and go to the store knowing what they want to purchase, which will be driving, which will be driving traditional retailers to be more competitive and innovative in attracting and retaining customers. As mentioned, today's toy buyers are much more informed about the products they are looking for, and that trend is only going to continue. Online research is also having an impact on the number of times a consumer goes to the store, and the amount of time he or she spends there, which is already having an impact on unplanned purchases, as we've seen over the past several years. Brick and mortar stores are going to have to do a better job of making their toy departments a consumer destination.

Where this will have a strong positive impact is on the smaller companies and retailers who will be able to use online to leverage visibility and sales they might not get otherwise. Retailers are already looking for toys that they can sell exclusively online, either because of space limitations or because they serve a more narrow demographic than their key customers—and they don't want to leave money on the table if they have the option not to. This effectively levels the playing field for smaller companies because, again, this is a product driven business, and one never really knows where the next great product is going to come from.

As we saw at the outset, the traditional toy industry has remained constant in its size for the past 10 years, and there is no reason to think that will change any time soon. Though children have given up playing with many traditional toys at a younger age than they did in the 1960s, 1970s and even 1980s, the process of child development is such that you're not going to see a newborn on a tablet computer, and there is reason to think that the so-called age compression has reached as far as it will go.

Toys will always be responsive to the marketplace, and one thing that can be predicted without any reservation is that toys will continue to reflect the culture, the trends of the time and the aspirations of children. Oh, and that successful toys will all have one thing in common: fun for the kids who love them.

# Bibliography

The Toy Industry Association. (n.d.). Retrieved from http://www.toy-tia.org

Consumer Product Safety Commission. (n.d.). Retrieved from http://www.cpsc.gov

Children's Online Privacy Protection. (n.d.). Retrieved from http://www.coppa.org

ICTI (International Council of Toy Industries). (n.d.). Retrieved from http://www.icti-care.org

ASTRA (Specialty toys). (n.d.). Retrieved from http://www.astratoy.org

## Toy Companies

Toy Directory—www.toydirectory.com
Mattel—www.mattel.com
Hasbro—www.hasbro.com
LeapFrog—www.leapfrog.com
Jakks Pacific—www.jakks.com
Spin Master—www.spinmaster.com

# Index

## A
Action Figure
  current market behavior, 20–22
  history, 16–18
  market status, 18–20
  *vs.* transformers, 23–27
Advertising
  television, 113–117
  traditional, 117
American International Toy Fair, 81
Arts and Crafts
  history, 27–28
  market status, 28–30
  succeed factors, 30
Auditing, 105–106

## B
Baby dolls, 38
Building and construction toys
  history, 31–32
  market status, 32–35
  succeed factors, 35–36

## C
CARU. *See* Children's Advertising Review Unit
Celebrity dolls, 96
Children's Advertising Review Unit (CARU), 116
Collectible dolls
  history, 47–48
  succeed factors, 48

## D
Dolls
  baby dolls, 38
  collectible dolls
    history, 47–48
    succeed factors, 48
  fashion dolls, 42–43
  feature dolls, 39–40
  history, 36–37
  large dolls, 38–39
  market status, 38
  mini dolls, 40–42
Dragon Tales toys, 60

## E
Exclusives, purchase decisions, 89–90

## F
Fads, purchase decisions, 90–91
Fantasy Play, 46
Fashion dolls, 42–43
FCC. *See* Federal Communications Commission
Feature dolls, 39–40
Federal Communications Commission (FCC), 115–116
Financial structure, toy industry, 127–135

## G
Games
  history, 48–50
  market status, 50–52
  succeed factors, 52–54
Grown-Up Play, 46–47

## I
Infant toys
  history, 56–57
  market status, 57–59
  succeed factors, 59–60
International Council of Toy Industries, 77

## L
Large dolls, 38–39
Licensing, 101–102
  brands, 111–112
  content, 118–119

final words, 112–113
movie properties, 110–111
online marketing, 117–118
television shows, 111
TV advertising, 113–117
Licensing Industries Merchandisers'
Association, 112

## M

Manufacturing, products, 77–78
Marketing process, 100–101
   audit provisions, 105–106
   distribution channels, 103–104
   licensing, 101–102
   minimum guarantee, 104–105
   product categories, 103
   product development, 106–107
   property selection, 107–109
   release dates, 103
   royalty rates, 105
   sell-off period, 106
   slice-ensing, 103
   upfront payment, 104–105
Mini dolls, 40–42
Money game, 127–135
Monster High, 43–47
Movie properties, licensing, 110–111

## N

New York Toy Fair, 81

## O

Online marketing, 117–118
Outdoor toys
   history, 60–61
   market status, 61
   succeed factors, 61–62

## P

Pictionary, 54–55
Plush toys
   history, 62
   market status, 63–64
   succeed factors, 64
Preschool toys
   history, 56–57

   market status, 57–59
   succeed factors, 59–60
Products
   general notes, 69–70
   internal development *vs.* inventors, 71–72
   manufacturing, 77–78
   objective of concept, 70–71
   production, 76–77
   prototypes, 74–76
   strategies for launching, 93–94
   testing, 76–77
   validation, 72–74
Prototypes, 74–76
Purchase decisions
   exclusives, 89–90
   exit strategy, 86–88
   fads, 90–91
   margins, 84–86
   market down, 88–89
   retail sectors, 89
   specialty market, 91–93
Puzzles
   history, 48–50
   market status, 50–52
   succeed factors, 52–54

## S

Sell-off period, 106
Slice-ensing, 103
Sports toys
   history, 60–61
   market status, 61
   succeed factors, 61–62

## T

Teenage Play, 47
Testing, products, 76–77
Toy categories
   Action Figure
      current market behavior, 20–22
      history, 16–18
      market status, 18–20
      *vs.* transformers, 23–27
   Arts and Crafts
      history, 27–28
      market status, 28–30

# INDEX

succeed factors, 30
baby dolls, 38
building and construction toys
   history, 31–32
   market status, 32–35
   succeed factors, 35–36
collectible dolls
   history, 47–48
   succeed factors, 48
description, 13–16
dolls
   history, 36–37
   market status, 38
fashion dolls, 42–43
feature dolls, 39–40
games and puzzles
   history, 48–50
   market status, 50–52
   succeed factors, 52–54
infant and preschool toys
   history, 56–57
   market status, 57–59
   succeed factors, 59–60
large dolls, 38–39
mini dolls, 40–42
Monster High, 43–47
other toys, 67–68
outdoor and sports toys
   history, 60–61
   market status, 61
   succeed factors, 61–62
Pictionary, 54–55
plush toys
   history, 62
   market status, 63–64
   succeed factors, 64
Transformers
   *vs.* action figure, 23–27
   description, 22–23
vehicle toys
   history, 64–66
   market status, 66–67
Toy companies, 141
Toy consumer, 99–100
Toy dollar, 12, 97–99
Toy Fair, 81–84
Toy industry
   current status, 5–8
   financial structure, 127–135
   growth, 2–3
   industrial evolution, 1–2
   post–wars years, 3–5
   rolling report, 10–11
Traditional advertising, 117
Transformers
   *vs.* action figure, 23–27
   description, 22–23
TV advertising, 113–117

## V

Validation, products, 72–74
Vehicle toys
   history, 64–66
   market status, 66–67

**OTHER TITLES IN OUR INDUSTRY PROFILES COLLECTION**

Donald Stengel, California State University, Fresno, Editor

- *A Profile of the Steel Industry: Global Reinvention for a New Economy* by Peter Warrian
- *A Profile of the Furniture Manufacturing Industry: Global Restructuring* by Susan M Walcott
- *A Profile of the Oil and Gas Industry: Resources, Market Forces, Geopolitics, and Technology* by Linda Herkenhoff
- *A Profile of the Farm Machinery Industry: Helping Farmers Feed the World* by Dawn Drake
- *A Profile of the Automobile and Motor Vehicle Industry: Innovation, Transformation, Globalization* 12/31/2013 by James M Rubenstein and Thomas H. Klier
- *A Profile of the U.S. Film Industry: From Content to Media to the World* 1/31/2014 by John W. Clarry
- *A Profile of the Wine Industry: Global, Local, Earth, and Glitz* 2/15/2014 by Barbara Insel
- *A Profile of the Textile Manufacturing Industry* 2/15/2014 by Erin Parrish
- *A Profile of the Performing Arts Industry: Culture and Commerce* 4/15/2014 by David H. Gaylin

## Announcing the Business Expert Press Digital Library

*Concise E-books Business Students*
*Need for Classroom and Research*

This book can also be purchased in an e-book collection by your library as
- a one-time purchase,
- that is owned forever,
- allows for simultaneous readers,
- has no restrictions on printing, and
- can be downloaded as PDFs from within the library community.

Our digital library collections are a great solution to beat the rising cost of textbooks. e-books can be loaded into their course management systems or onto student's e-book readers.

The **Business Expert Press** digital libraries are very affordable, with no obligation to buy in future years. For more information, please visit **www.businessexpertpress.com/librarians**. To set up a trial in the United States, please contact **Adam Chesler** at *adam.chesler@businessexpertpress.com* for all other regions, contact **Nicole Lee** at *nicole.lee@igroupnet.com*.

www.ingramcontent.com/pod-product-compliance
Lightning Source LLC
Chambersburg PA
CBHW070550170426
43201CB00012B/1791